Joel Shoemaker   12-88

Revolutionary Writings

Camilo Torres

Revolutionary Writings

Herder and Herder

1969
HERDER AND HERDER NEW YORK
232 Madison Avenue, New York, N.Y. 10016

Original edition: *Camilo Torres,*
Cuernavaca, Centro Intercultural de Documentación, 1966.
Translated by Robert Olsen and Linda Day.

CONTENTS

Revolutionary Writings

I.
THE MODERN UNIVERSITY
AND SOCIAL PROBLEMS

1. The Role of the University

It has always been the role of the university to educate and train a country's leaders, whether from the scientific point of view or the ethical. In the various fields of science, the future professionals acquire the indispensable knowledge for investigating and solving the specific problems of their country and their society. From the ethical point of view, the instruction is dual. Negatively, the students are taught to use this knowledge without impairing or lessening the rights of God and men. Positively, their scientific concerns are oriented primarily towards the service of God and neighbor rather than the service of self alone.

This double instruction is deeply rooted not only in the principles of revelation but also in those of simple natural reason. Through revelation we know that to love God and neighbor is the greatest commandment. We also know that we are tempting God if we try to attain an end without using the most appropriate means to do this. Now then, to love is to serve, and the best way to serve is through science. Natural reason tells us that science must regard man, conceived in all his fullness, as its end and purpose. Science is inconceivable apart from the service of man and of God perceived through man.

Moreover, serving the common good, even at the cost of self-sacrifice, is neither sincere nor effective if no attempt is made to seek the best means. The service of man cannot be conceived without scientific and technical methods. Especially in our Latin

American countries in which the disproportion between the development of the material elements with respect to the development of the human elements is greater, the urgency of human development is more pressing.

2. Social Problems in Relation to Science and Service

All service is intrinsically social, presupposing at least two individuals. In this respect, ethical instruction has necessarily been social, and similarly—although perhaps not for the same reason—scientific instruction has always had to be social also, and of course there could be no moral education without speculative learning. Furthermore, the scientific instruction of the universities has been oriented down through the years in accordance with the needs and concerns of every era. This is the only way to produce leaders who respond to the historical vocation which calls them to action and achievement in each era.

It is axiomatic to say that the problems which most insistently demand solution and which most concern modern man are social problems. Both national and international politics are now oriented in accordance with them. The various sciences—medicine, engineering, architecture, psychology, economics, and so forth—are laying more and more emphasis upon social aspects and implications.

The world is awakening from a long individualistic stupor and now concentrates upon society. It is impossible, therefore, that the university, which is educating and training the leaders of various countries, should fail to prepare them for adequate solution of the great contemporary problems. The university would betray its mission if it produced professional leaders uninterested in man, society, and God. This interest cannot be imbued in our day without revealing the profound causes of modern human problems and the social needs that demand prompt solution.

3. The Study of Social Problems

These problems have long been studied. In recent years, however, the field of study has been increasingly specified and divided. Its division between speculative and positive social sciences has clarified many problems and perfected the methods also. Sociology considers itself to be a science of positive observation, independent of social philosophy, which is a normative science. Consequently, many sociological investigations undertaken by persons of different and adverse ideologies can and must coincide if they have been carried out with full scientific rigor.

This distinction does not imply disconnection. The normative factor must enter into the phase of action. It is important, therefore, that the norm be in accordance with reality, and that reality be adequately known. But this adequate knowledge cannot be acquired without scientific research. Consequently, it is indispensable that all social action be based upon the positive investigation of reality in addition to the doctrinal basis.

This means that universities cannot refuse to consider the problem of social inquiry. Social problems are certainly concrete, and their forms depend upon the particular culture and society. Therefore, the attempt to propose principles without any application to a clearly determined national reality would not greatly contribute to the well-being of our country. Professors of the positive social sciences must necessarily base their courses upon the concrete investigations that have been made.

4. Concern for Social Problems

Real concern for social problems requires a minimal basis of altruism. This altruism must be founded upon solid principles and then must be adequately sustained if it is to be put into practice. Christian insight and awareness, insofar as it is wholly based on love, is the best source of altruism, not only in the ordinary, minimal sense, but also in the heroic degree which is manifested in the history of the Church.

The sustenance of this attitude and outlook, in addition to the human principle of Christian love, consists in the supernatural life of grace, which sustains man in his weakness and makes him both dependable and zealous. That is why religious education is necessary in a Catholic country like ours, strictly from the point of view of social problems. To really provide for this, there should be a priest in each faculty of the social sciences.

The fact that social concern coalesces so perfectly with Christian concern implicitly indicates the prudence which Catholics must possess and practice in regard to social questions. They should know to what extent they can and should acquiesce. Insofar as these sciences—when they are positive—are based upon research, it is necessary to determine the degree of validity and effectiveness of the research, and then to try to distinguish the positive aspect it contains. It is also indispensable to see the possible scientific and theological weaknesses in order to be capable of defending these perspectives in a field that is open to them both.

We see how necessary it is for university chaplains to be informed about social questions. They should orient the judgment and outlook of all Catholic students who, in turn, must then influence others. Finally, it is most important that religious problems be stated and combined with those of science in the most rational manner, fully in accordance with scientific thought and outlook. The full explanation of the social implications of the Gospel will be the method used to carry out this dual effort. Accordingly, university chaplains must be imbued with passionate concern for the same problems that are of interest to students, and must integrate this concern within a vital Christian faith.

5. Recommendations

1. Ask the Venerable Episcopal Conference to approve a proposal appointing certain full-time priests to provide spiritual ministration to university students of the whole country.

2. Create an interuniversity Institute of Social Research to provide research programs and research scholars for the various faculties of social sciences that are functioning in this country.

II.
THE STANDARD OF LIVING IN BOGOTÁ

Introduction

It has long been commonplace to speak of the poverty that is characteristic of the slum districts of all the big, modern cities, and more especially of cities located in developing countries. However, it is difficult, in statistical terms, to prove the veracity of this impression of poverty which our urban centers convey. Demagogues and revolutionaries lay great stress upon this, but it may be nothing more than a limited and isolated phenomenon of the problems pertaining to the socio-economic structure of a country.

For these reasons it does not seem superfluous to try to trace to some extent the phenomenon of "poverty" in the city of Bogotá. This present treatise is a chapter of the thesis presented by the author to the University of Louvain in 1958. But no attempt has been made to set forth a complete explication of the phenomenon of poverty in Bogotá. The only purpose is to interpret the statistical sources on which we rely in Colombia. We shall try to encompass this interpretation within the socio-economic explanations of the urban phenomenon in developing countries, especially in our Latin American countries.

The lack of a process of gestation is one of the characteristics of socio-economic change in Latin America. As subsidiaries of the European world in our culture and institutions, Latin Americans have received rather than generated the new economic, social, and political systems. This reception has generally occurred in a wholly indiscriminate manner, with no respect for

16

the existing culture and no process of assimilation. Consequently, Latin American society is the victim of specific traumas which add to the acuteness of the situations of tension and social conflict which must be coped with in any induced social change. Among these tensions and conflicts we want to enumerate some which, although not exclusively Latin American, are more intensely manifested on this continent because of the lack of an assimilative process. We have also chosen the following examples as the basis of urban problems in developing regions.

1. Proletarization

The existing correlation between proletarization and urbanization is well known. However, this is not sufficient to clearly determine the scope of these concepts. Proletarization may be considered as the process whereby a great proportion of wage-earners are barred from every means of livelihood other than their own labor. Consequently, proletarization presupposes a socio-economic structure based upon the division of labor, the concentration of capital, and industrialization. These are elements which in fact coincided with the birth of the large modern cities. As a result of the human concentration required by the division of labor and industrialization, a concentration of services took place. Accordingly, although industrialization is a phenomenon more economic than social, and differs from urbanization, which is more social than economic, both generally occur in parallel form.

The phenomenon of proletarization has been partly controlled in its process in industrialized countries. The cogent practice of concentrating capital by lowering wages had to be stopped for economic reasons (as, for instance, the decreasing yield and profit of invested capital), and for social reasons (for example, the vindictive attitude of the proletariat). There were also legal reasons (expressed in social legislation), institutional determinants (labor unions, coordinating commissions, arbitration, mediation, and so forth), and, of course, political factors (the rise of industrial democracy, and so forth).

Additionally, in the industrial countries the increase of labor's productivity through mechanization and automation, and by greater occupational skills, has considerably increased the earnings of the workers. We know that higher wages enable the workers to save money, even if they also result in greater demand for consumer necessities. This is what has occurred in countries that are already industrialized.

Moreover, the ownership of private property in an industrial society does not constitute the only element of prestige and security. The new social institutions can guarantee this prestige and security quite independently of the possession of private property. This is apparent in both socialist and capitalist countries.

All of these factors, and many others also, indicate a regression of the process of proletarization in the industrialized countries.

On the other hand, in the developing countries the phenomenon of proletarization is increasing, although industrialization and the concentration of capital are still in their initial stage. The productivity of labor is still very low in relation to the industrialized nations. And consequently, real wages and savings are diminishing rather than rising.

In view of the system of values, which is still at the feudal level, and the lack of other institutions, private property in our countries, even in the cities, constitutes the principal element of prestige and security. And since private property is a form of savings, the lack of property increases proletarization by dispossessing the worker.

2. Factors of Rural Emigration

The increase of urban population is a world-wide phenomenon (cf. *The Demographic Yearbook of the United Nations*). The rate of natural growth of rural population, and consequently

18

the demographic predominance of the city over the country, can only be explained by rural immigration to the cities.

Among the factors which demographers and sociologists have indicated as causes of the exodus from the country and the attraction of the city in any society (cf. E. Bugel, *Urban Sociology* [New York, Toronto, and London, 1955], pp. 211–262), we shall note those which possess special importance in Latin America.

ELEMENTS OF THE CITY'S ATTRACTION

The "urban mirage" which attracts country-dwellers when the contrast between city and country is great, is all the stronger always and whenever this contrast can be clearly perceived. In Latin America, because the process of assimilating the elements of an industrial society is lacking, the contrasts produced between the rural and urban environments are even greater. Within just a few miles we can encounter elements of a pre-Colombian culture and elements of the most advanced civilization of our time. The economic, social, and cultural differences between city and country are immensely greater than those existing in the developed nations.

With regard to the means of communication, the difference is not so great. It is easier to establish radio, telegraph, television, movies, and newspapers in rural areas than to raise the standard of living or provide services of any kind. Therefore, immigration to the city is produced more easily not only because the contrast is greater, but because the contrast may be made more easily than the rural inhabitants may realize.

ELEMENTS OF THE EXODUS
FROM THE COUNTRY

The standard of living is low in rural areas, and yet we know that these areas, in the underdeveloped countries, have the greatest natural growth of population in the world. Agrarian reforms in the underdeveloped countries, and more especially in Latin America, have been the order in present-day interest and concern.

All of this clearly indicates the anomalies in the economic structure of our rural regions, resulting in the low standard of living of the rural population. Country people find themselves obligated to seek new sources of income in the urban areas. The lack of services and entertainment, the difficulties and ruggedness of country life, all impel our rural inhabitants to try to emigrate, even more so than in the developed countries. Further, in some countries, as in Colombia for instance, we have the phenomenon of violence, especially in the rural areas. Country-dwellers, as in feudal times, seek safety and security in the cities.

3. Qualitative Characteristics of Urban Immigration

In European countries we encounter the phenomenon of industrialization following upon a greatly increased handicraft production, which prepared skilled workers for the industrial revolution. In Latin America, however, there was no significant growth in handicraft. Nor was there any important urban concentration of craftsmen. Finally, there was no scarcity of manual labor, which might have induced mechanization.

Industry in Latin America has always lacked skilled workers. And rural immigration enlarged the ranks of unskilled workers whose excessive number produced apparent or concealed unemployment typical of our urban centers. The phenomenon of unemployment gets worse in those cities which are predominantly administrative, commercial, and cultural, with specialization in the tertiary sector of production—the services of all kinds.

Occasionally, these services may exercise a power of attraction upon country-dwellers. Moreover, we know that the development of the tertiary sector is disproportionate, in our countries, in relation to the secondary sector engaged in the transformation of

20

products. Therefore, the masses of rural immigrants meet with conditions that are even more unfavorable when they arrive in a city that is predominantly tertiary. They cannot be absorbed by industry because they are unskilled, and even fewer can be absorbed into the class of salaried employees. The personal services, which include shoe-shining, domestic service, and cartage, in the manner of concealed unemployment, constitute the occupational sector of refuge.

This seems to be the situation in Bogotá. Established as a religious, cultural, administrative, and military center, it attracted an abundant rural immigration when there were possibilities of contact and of social exchange induced in behalf of the city in the rural areas. Proportionately to other cities, Bogotá is much more tertiary than secondary. Industry has never been able to absorb all the unskilled workers who come to the city. They increase consumption, of course. But they do not acquire any regular or customary industrial consumption until after a process of assimilation to city life.

III.
LAND EXPLOITATION
AND LAND REFORM

1. Agrarian Reform

It is already a truism to say that we cannot even think of a simple partition of lands that does not include technical assistance and education. I also believe that it is important to lay stress upon the distinction existing between agrarian reform and colonization. Naturally, in a country like ours and in most Latin American countries, there is much unexploited land which is not developed because of the difficulties that it would entail. On the other hand, we must confront the two great problems of small and large landholdings which bear on the central question of agrarian reform and which are fundamental elements in the exploitation of land. These landholdings constitute an inherited patrimony of the landholders which certainly calls for a redistribution of all such land that is now productive or could at least become so.

If we are truly sincere, we cannot consider an agrarian reform based merely upon unexploited or unexploitable land, but rather upon the land which is already cultivated, constituting an important source of production for the country. Simple partition would lower production, as occurred in all other countries, but if there is also a division and sharing of credit, technical assistance, and agricultural or cooperative education, there would probably be a real remedy. This is naturally more complicated, but I believe that it would be more realistic.

First of all, I want to comment on the remarks of Dr. Castellanos concerning the position of the landholding class in regard to agrarian reform. I believe that if we circumscribe the concept of agrarian reform in such a way as to include technical matters and the increase of production, the utilization of lands, and transportation and marketing facilities, we must principally consider the partition of land that is already productive or which can again become productive.

It was with regard to this last concept that I have mentioned the resistance of the landholding class to agrarian reform. This does not mean that individuals cannot separately agree to land partition, but that landholders as a whole, and acting as a social group, will have to act in terms of their common interests. And it is precisely against these common interests that the partition of productive land would be carried out.

With reference to the question of cooperatives, it seems obvious to me, from the economic point of view, that if one of the bases of agrarian reform is the multiplication of the number of producers, it would be economically harmful if at the same time we could not organize an association to cope with the general expenditures of these many producers. Because of the division of land ownership, this could only be achieved with the help of cooperative procedures and practices.

Naturally, the cooperative must not be regarded merely as an economic system, because it is primarily an educational method which prepares individuals to sacrifice their particular interests for the sake of the collectivity. And obviously, a cooperative of isolated production alone would not be satisfactory. Necessarily, it must be combined or connected with cooperatives of transport and consumption in order to complete the cycle of economic production and distribution. I believe, therefore, that cooperatives must form the basis of agrarian reform.

2. The Landholding Class

I believe that a discussion of this kind, as any attempt to speak the truth, has clarified and summarized many points. And consequently, I feel that we have at least reached a point of theoretical agreement. In my opinion, the polemical aspect can be summed up in a classical sociological problem pertaining to the relations of man and the land, and of man and property ownership. If we accept a determinism of property and ownership over man's behavior in general, we could be accused of a Marxist and unilateralist point of view. And if we accept the determinism of humanity over the economic factor, with complete independence of the latter, we would be utopian idealists. As Christians we must accept man in his fullness—body and soul, matter and spirit, the socio-economic factor and the human factor.

Man's effect upon property is sufficiently clear to indicate the indispensable necessity of education and technical training, communal association and organization in general. The influence of private property on the behavior of the individual is of no less importance. The problem of insecurity in regard to life and the future, the ability to increase production and one's standard of living, and to improve one's education and social prestige, all depend very directly upon possession of the means of production.

In theory, we have reached this agreement. And we have the consolation of hearing Dr. Castellanos, as a representative of the landholding class, assure us that members of this class would not object to a partition of productive land. I hope that when it comes to putting this plan into practice the group which he represents will act more in terms of collective interests than for the sake of selfish interests alone.

Whenever I have referred to the landholding class, I have not intended in any way to do this in terms of a Marxist criterion or of struggle between classes. I have only wanted to express the sociological reality. A social class, conceived scientifically, is a union of individuals who form a group possessing common interests, values, and motivations, with awareness of this common bond. This awareness is manifested in institutions like those mentioned by Dr. Aguilera Camacho, organized as guilds, associations, or trade unions which represent and defend the interests of every class or subordinate class.

3. Reform for Colombia

I have been asked about agrarian reform in other countries and the possibility of utilizing these experiments advantageously. Perhaps there are positive elements in these experiments. However, we must not copy them simply because they were successfully tried in other environments. I believe that we have already experienced harsh results because we transplanted foreign institutions indiscriminately, without taking into account our local reality.

All experiments should be fully investigated, but they can only be useful to us insofar as they correspond to the specific conditions of our own national environment. In order to really know these conditions, we must undertake serious scientific inquiries. Our planning should be expressed in terms of this scientific knowledge and carried out in view of the greatest effectiveness in all of our programs. If these solutions occasionally coincide with those adopted in Cuba, Mexico, China, and Bolivia, or any other country in the world, it should be of no importance to us because we are not adopting them on account of any such similarity, but simply because they correspond to objective local necessities.

IV.
STRUCTURING AN AUTHENTIC
LATIN AMERICAN SOCIOLOGY

1. Cultural Colonialism
in Latin America

Latin American culture, to say the least, is but little institution-alized. It consists in unintegrated patterns and other patterns which, although they constituted an indigenous cultural patri-mony, have now disappeared. The coexistence of assimilated ele-ments and uncultured elements has led many sociologists and anthropologists to question the very existence of an authentic Latin American culture in the strict sense.

Among the newer cultural elements is sociology, regarded as a science and a method. In the chronicles of the Indian tribes, of course, we find real sociological and anthropological analyses. However, sociology considered as a structured branch of science was not cultivated until the end of the last century and the early years of the twentieth. Admittedly, this has not always remained within the norms of a scientific sociology, but at least the name of sociology as a science has been utilized.

And it is undeniable that the new discipline has constituted an important and foreign cultural element. The many sociological schools in the United States and Europe will find their repre-sentatives in Latin America functioning more as copyists than as interpreters of these schools. Sociology has not been an exception within the mosaic of our cultural colonialism which persists along with our economic and political colonialism. In view of the rather foreign character of these cultural importations, their development in Latin American countries is largely subsidiary to the direction and timing of development in the countries of other continents.

Accordingly, the positive and empirical conception of sociology did not become widespread in Latin America until after the last World War, with several years of delay in relation to Europe, and more especially with regard to Anglo-Saxon sociology. And it was adopted as an imported conception and not as a culmination of a scientific process achieved by the "intelligentsia" of our countries. Nevertheless, the new orientation implies a scientific projection upon our own social order. Positive science cannot isolate itself from a concrete local environment. Much less is this possible in the case of a social science. Studies concerning our society are beginning to multiply. Professional sociologists trained in Europe and the United States are now appearing in all of our countries. At the Sixth Latin American Congress of Sociology, held this year in Caracas, there was already much talk about the triumph of the professional sociologists over simple amateurs. The reports and essays on positive research were quite numerous. Official recognition of positive sociology in Latin America could now at last be proclaimed. In spite of all this, however, scientific parasitism has not yet been eliminated. We have combined the faults of extra-continental sociology with its good qualities. The structuring of an authentic Latin American sociology still seems to be in very embryonic form.

2. The Danger of "Nominalism"

With regard to the most common faults, I would like to refer only to one, nominalism, because it is universally prevalent in sociology and is closely related to the unauthentic aspects which we shall now consider. When I speak of "nominalism," I mean, for instance, the use of words that are not strictly connected with the personal observations of the individual using them. Nominalism places greater emphasis on terminology than on observation of reality. It is the course of least resistance for the professional person in appearing to possess a real science when in fact his only possession is a scientific vocabulary. This phenomenon has justified the assertion of those who say that sociology resembles a man who, with complicated and unintelligible words, speaks of things that everyone knows by common sense. Nominalism is such a tempting field for mediocrity that quite possibly in very few years we shall see our continent overrun with pseudo-scientists who possess a sociological jargon, but who are unable to observe our social order in its reality, or synthesize their observations and generalize the characteristics of this reality in systematic form.

It is essential that all of us who engage in teaching and training the Latin American sociologists of the future should be fully aware of this great danger that threatens our sociology. We must utilize a realistic pedagogical method that is intransigent in giving absolute priority to immediate observation over the use of an empty and meaningless terminology. Otherwise, we might frustrate the contribution of a positive sociology. We would diminish the sense of realistic delineation of the typical social phenomena of our continent which this science claims for itself now that it is guided by an empirical method. Perhaps this insistence upon down-to-earth methods and practices, and the combating of irrational rote learning in our students, may help us in this realistic purification of our future professionals. In any case, this is a problem of method which ought to assume a primary place in our academic concerns.

3. The Authenticity of Latin American Sociology

We have heard much argument about the legitimacy of the geographical specification of a science. But how can we distinguish North American mathematics from Soviet mathematics, except in reference to the nationality of the mathematicians? The same problem arises in connection with the positive conception of the social sciences. According as methods are standardized and generalizations are established which can be verified empirically, the social sciences, and especially sociology, rise above the philosophical, religious, cultural, and geographical frontiers, and acquire a universal citizenship in unison with the other modern sciences. Nevertheless, in regard to subject matter the social sciences differ from the other positive sciences. The geographical element, or rather the ecology, is an essential element in the total consideration of a social complex. Consequently, the geographical specification is not detrimental to the universality of a science. With regard to sociology, we can affirm that it cannot be called "American," "European," or "Latin American" as far as general methods and universal laws are concerned. However, the religious problematic is different. Social dynamics and structures have specific modalities within every culture and subculture. In a word, we can speak in terms of a Latin American sociology insofar as its object is the analysis and interpretation of the problems and the typical situations of our regional areas, and to the extent that it must apply methods and theories to these problems and specific situations.

We must now consider two dangers in the structuring of a typically Latin American sociology. The first danger could be called a cowardice or timidity disguised as objectivity, and the second danger is a demagogy concealed by apparent scientific significance.

TIMIDITY DISGUISED AS OBJECTIVITY

The strong insistence upon objectivity is fully justifiable among the concerns and interests of any scientist, but in view of previous experience, and especially in the concerns of the Latin American sociologist, there have been too many disappointments derived from theoretical, normative, and objective sociology, so propitious to our Latin mind, resulting in a distrust of the effort to bring our social reality into focus. Our society is a fermenting source of immediate problems of all kinds in which we necessarily find ourselves involved with our affectivity, our intellect, and our whole person. It is easy indeed to allow ourselves to be impressed by the objectivism in social analyses. All of this justifies the desire to maintain a cool scientific objectivity in our sociological work.

Nevertheless, all social problems must be the object of the sociologist's consideration and study. An *a priori* discrimination between problems that ought to be studied and those which ought not to be studied is certainly not a scientific attitude. Moreover, if any of the more obvious problems are among those we exclude, we are then stunting the growth of our field of knowledge, depriving it of objectives which might be definitive and conclusive for complete scientific integration.

It seems to me that in this attitude there is an element of professional deontology which we cannot overlook. In my opinion, the scientist should not make an abstraction of his total human personality, except insofar as the purposes of science are obstructed by elements of this personality. This occurs, for instance, in value judgments. However, I believe that it would be detrimental to authentic scientific achievement if all the wealth of the scientist's human personality were discarded, even though this wealth is not an element that we can classify as strictly methodological. Imagination, intuition, general culture, idealism, and generosity are imponderable and qualitative factors which sometimes define what we mean when we speak of a scientist. Among these "existential" elements, so to speak, is the determination to enter into the difficult questions and problems of our time and the concrete society in which we live. To omit the problematical questions of our time and of our Latin American society from our sociological objectives could only be justified scientifically at the risk of losing objectivity. However, we can properly ask ourselves a few questions. Do we not already possess a sufficiently standardized methodology? Is human communication not sufficiently extensive to allow for universal criticism?

Can we not hope for a scientific education that will enable us to take up those problems whose omission would leave a transcendental gap in our conception of Latin American reality? Are the controls of scientific objectivity in sociology still so rudimentary that we must deprive ourselves of whatever seems most interesting among our social problems?

If the answer to this last question were affirmative, the classification of sociology as a science would be very questionable. As sociologists, we would have to limit ourselves to the study of non-transcendental problems as the only way to be objective. But it seems to me that the present development of sociology places us in a more optimistic position. I believe that we can affirm, from the scientific point of view, that there are not sufficient reasons to refuse consideration of those problems which matter most to our society. Those problems include social revolution, social change, the sociological effects of agrarian reform, the development of community, and the expansion of imperialism, and those should constitute the present agenda of study for Latin American sociologists.

DEMAGOGY CONCEALED BY "SCIENTIFIC SIGNIFICANCE"

In countries where immediate problems are most pressing there is less development of research, reflection, and planning. This phenomenon is logical, but it means that the institutions are not functioning properly. And it is precisely those countries that are most in need of planning that have it in least adequate form.

A strict scientific asceticism is essential to avoid being completely overwhelmed by the immediate need for action and to devote the time required for research. It is this pressure of immediate needs that spreads the idea that research is secondary and action primary. Without engaging in Byzantine discussions concerning values and priorities, we can say that research and planning, which are both very necessary, are difficult to fully carry out in countries whose immediate needs call for immediate action, as in our Latin American countries. This phenomenon is especially obvious in regard to social matters, and here we find that research scholars are lacking while politicians increase. The polemical, emotional writings on social problems and social policy become more abundant, to the detriment of properly scientific literature.

Those who call themselves "sociologists" are beginning to be victimized by the pressure of urgency and immediacy. The position of the "timid scientists" which we have mentioned provides them with arguments for abandoning research and for doubting objectivity. Their chosen themes, although expressed in very impartial and objective form, appear as shields of defense for non-scientific interests of class, or economic and political interests. This position of doubt with regard to objectivity on the part of sociologists who belong to a particular social class and are rooted within a particular political and social system, in addition to being stimulated by the attitudes of the "timid scientists," is guided and governed by the dogmatism of the false disciples of Marx and Engels, and I shall try to explain what is meant by "false disciples."

According to these disciples, there ought to be a proletarian sociology and a bourgeois sociology. Similarly, they speak of proletarian art and bourgeois art, and even proletarian and bourgeois genetics and mathematics! In other words, they say that class conditioning is total and absolute, and that no scientist is exempt from it.

Naturally, we cannot deny that such conditioning exists. The "timid scientists" are a proof of its existence. But we cannot agree that this conditioning is total in all individuals. Both Marx and Engels themselves had sufficiently penetrating analytical minds to realize this. They described and foresaw the attitude of a minority of the "ruling class" that would oppose the interests of this same class. They utilized this minority for their revolutionary purposes, although at least in the case of Engels they did not personally belong to the proletariat. Nevertheless, they claimed to be the authentic spokesmen of this class. This indicates that Marx and Engels were not as absolute as some of their disciples in upholding the notion of class conditioning. If they could allow for exceptions in a field in which objectivity is more difficult—notably the field of politics—why do their disciples refuse to allow any exceptions in the strictly defined field of science?

This is not to say that we want to disregard the influence which belonging to a class or particular group can exert upon the attitudes of any individual. We would no longer be sociologists if we did not affirm this influence. Neither can we deny that withdrawal from social influences is quite common today. But we have reference to exceptions, and these can only be obtained on the basis of scientific discipline and training, moral values and professional ethics, self-criticism and recognition of suitable value judgments, thus protecting and ensuring integrity in the investigation of facts. And to become an exception of this kind is fundamental to becoming a scientist. That is why it is difficult to find authentic scientists. And that is why a real sociologist must also be an exception. Another stimulus is combined with anterior motivations so that our sociologists abandon the high road of scientific objectivity, or else become doubtful about it, and then devote themselves wholly to action or political literature. That stimulus is the temptation of popularity.

For many sociologists it is a harsh trial to see impartial analyses, although pertaining to urgent problems, producing less enthusiasm, even among intellectuals, than demagogical elucidations. The motives are obvious, but the reaction of the scientists is no less real. The apparent "loss of popularity" leaves a certain nostalgic longing for demagogical prestige. It is difficult to resist this temptation. It is hard to reject a demagogical attitude or refuse to seek a scientific kind of rationalization to justify it. The course of least resistance is to indiscriminately blame all those who want to remain on the solid ground of objectivity, accusing them of scientific cowardice. We then try to conceal our demagogy with some excuse of scientific significance, withdrawing ourselves from the properly scientific terrain so that we can devote ourselves to political and demagogical activity.

4. The Education and Training
of Latin American Sociologists

There can be no science without scientists, and for the same reason no sociology can ever be authentically Latin American unless there are authentic Latin American sociologists. Those of us who have the responsibility of educating our future Latin American sociologists know that our task is great indeed. We must not let ourselves be deceived about this. We could be running the risk of preparing nominalists rather than scientists. We could be orientating our concerns and those of our students towards non-transcendental problems under the pretext of objectivity. We could fall into an anti-scientific demagogy under the pretext of moral value in our professional activity.

To tell the truth, we do not even have a clear conception of the meaning and significance of Latin American sociology. We need to make a scientific and systematic evaluation of it. We must prepare and plan a realistic and intelligent course to follow. I believe that it has become imperative and urgent to outline a sociology of Latin American sociology!

At the future meetings of Latin American sociologists these concrete problems ought to be faced. We should evaluate whatever is existent. And we must standardize our methods. We must also define the dangers and summarize the problems for purposes of research and teaching. It is possible that the future Latin American Congress of Sociology which will meet in Bogotá may be an appropriate instrument for the achievement of this task.

However, it is surely most important that our sociologists possess a sincere attitude of self-criticism in the light of present and local problems. This attitude should be disseminated in the schools, departments, institutes, and faculties of sociology in all the various countries. We must be imbued with respect for methods, research, teaching, and training. This attitude is the only guarantee that we shall some day accomplish the structuring of an authentic Latin American sociology.

V.
THE STRUCTURE AND ROLE
OF THE UNIVERSITY

1. *The Chaplain and the Rector*

The closure was motivated by the strike; the strike, by the cancellation of ten matriculations without preliminary hearings or any kind of investigation, and these disciplinary measures resulted from the street disturbances of June 6. The automatism of these chain reactions suggests that nobody in the University makes good use of intelligence.

There was the irresponsibility of President Lleras in handing over the public thoroughfare to an uncontrollable demonstration. Moreover, it should be noted that the leaders did not know how to obtain prudent maintenance of order or a respectful attitude of the students in regard to this matter. It was the rector's duty to pronounce sanctions, but only in regard to those students whose misconduct was proved, and not merely the ten students whom he considered "rebellious." And the Student Council, instead of taking over the park of the National University to celebrate "University Week," should have used all possible means of conciliation, respectfully persuading Ramirez Montufar that his sanctions were juridical aberrations. Finally, the academic administrators proceeded with absolute incomprehension to decide upon the closure, instead of utilizing the transaction efforts undertaken by the administrators and professors of the Faculty of Sociology.

Only one person explained the problem of the National University both clearly and courageously. And that was its chaplain, Father Camilo Torres, the eminent professor of sociology. He had written a declaration (summarized in our previous edition) which made it possible to cherish the hope of a peaceful solution. Sanctions were approved, but applied in proper form, with objective impersonal bases and without ideological persecution. Furthermore, the Dean of Sociology, Orlando Fals Borda, and almost all the professors of this faculty also signed the declaration. Likewise, not less than two hundred professors approved the decision to continue classes. But Ramirez Montufar, who had never before been notably excessive, called them "clowns" and threatened the definitive closure of the National University. It was understandable that in view of such recklessness, the students thought of designating Father Camilo Torres as rector, asking the assistance of all the professors and, finally, setting an example of responsibility, reopening classes by their own authority.

Unfortunately, this was not possible. The vow of obedience is binding upon Father Camilo. When he was asked by the Cardinal Primate to withdraw from the University, he could only submit his resignation.

2. The Crisis of the University

WHAT IS THE GENERAL ATTITUDE CONCERNING THE UNIVERSITY?

It is quite symptomatic that the problems of the National University are considered by society, the administrators, the professors, and even the students only in times of crisis. This may show us that there is no abiding interest in having a university that is truly worthy of the name. The periodic crises reveal an acute manifestation of chronic sickness.

Abandoning this attitude is essential if we are to seek a

fundamental solution. On the other hand, we could continue to administer sedatives when, in fact, we should have recourse to surgery. We could go on believing that sanctions applied in troublesome moments can take the place of the customary and continuing pedagogical process. Here we see the first great defect, and we must seek its cause. Why is there no enduring concern in considering the problems of the University?

However, crises perform a function that is quite significant. When they occur, the problems acquire a more protuberant dimension and then it is easier to detect them. To do this in a precise and objective way, it will be necessary to undertake an investigation as comprehensively as possible concerning the different incidents and affairs of the University. Dr. Robert Williamson of the Faculty of Sociology has already begun a general survey that could constitute the basis for other soundings. Nevertheless, some of the causes are so obvious that we could now definitely establish them.

WHAT IS THE PARTICULAR ATTITUDE OF THE STUDENTS AND THE ADMINISTRATORS?

It is an evident fact that the students of our University exercise much more initiative than the professors and administrators. This does not mean that these initiatives are always good. In fact, however, they almost always are, as for instance a petition to remove an incompetent professor, integration of the University budget, and solidarity in opposing an injustice. The purposes of the complaints and requests are not generally attacked or widely discussed because they are unknown by the public. All that is criticized are the methods employed, including violence, lockouts, strikes, and demonstrations.

If we learn that the objectives are often quite just but the methods are faulty, why do the administrators fail to take the initiative in the attainment of these objectives, using methods that are more institutionalized and normal? This raises another question that should be answered.

Nevertheless, if we accept this situation as factual, we might ask ourselves: If the administrators and professors are not ordinarily concerned about the fundamental problems of the University, and do not take the initiative regarding them, why is it that when students do so they will not try to orient their activity in keeping with the methods that ought to be employed?

DO THE STUDENTS LACK ORIENTATION IN THEIR ACTIVITIES?

Unfortunately, the students in their meetings, assemblies, and demonstrations resemble a flock of sheep without a shepherd. They seem to be completely abandoned to chance and fate, and to their own judgment and immaturity. The professors and administrators believe that there is nothing for them to do when the students assemble together to solve problems. But later, when the students, abandoned by their teachers, make immature decisions and engage in censurable acts, the professors and administrators point an implacable and accusing finger towards those whom they consider guilty or those who seem bothersome or annoying.

Why are there no professors to advise the students in moments of crisis? Is this not perhaps when they need counsel most? Possibly to avoid compromising themselves . . . , however, the deeper causes must still be examined.

In these preceding considerations we have discovered a major problem: the lack of administrative personnel, adequately qualified and employed full-time, who would think seriously about the problems of the University and be directly informed about them, while maintaining close contact with the students.

ARE THE PROFESSORS LACKING
DIDACTIC AUTHORITY?

To maintain sufficiently qualified personnel, they must be well paid. Apostles are unpredictable exceptions, and we cannot base a solid structure upon exceptions. At the present time it is difficult to offer good salaries because of budget deficiencies. These deficiencies are attributable not only to the amounts that are provided, but more especially to their distribution. An excessive and inefficient bureaucracy, and their ineffective standards for spending money, means that the greatest share of the budget cannot be used for payment of more qualified administrators. In spite of all this, the technical qualification of professors and administrators does not depend wholly upon remuneration. The criteria and standards of selection must be objective and adequate.

In selecting personnel, modern psychology utilizes means and methods that are quite perfected. But it is of major importance that the possibilities of being chosen should be extended to all Colombians and all professionals. That is why there must be national competitive examinations open to all those who want to obtain appointment to a professorship.

ARE THERE DEFECTS
IN THE STRUCTURE OF THE UNIVERSITY?

The formal structure of the University is important, but we know very well that any legal statutes can be operative with good personnel, and the best law can be frustrated if there is no one to apply it. The most important purpose of the law is precisely to permit a proficient selection of the administrators and professors.

In the present Organic Statute of the University the criteria of professional selection are predominantly subjective. And this accounts for the considerable importance of the controlling "clique" of every faculty. The appointment of professors, the approval of regulations and programs in general, and all the policies of each faculty, depend on each administrative council and every dean in the National University. The Academic Council is the supreme authority. But an authority shared by twenty-four deans tends towards anarchy or arbitrariness. This council works as a team only in regard to matters of very special interest, as for instance the University budget, which brings the members together to defend the interests of each faculty, or when someone's personal prestige is at stake among people who are not connected with the University. Decisions are then easily made without deliberation and are strictly determined by a desire to please public opinion, the government, or any other pressure group.

ARE "BUREAUCRACY" AND "CLIQUISM" OPERATIVE IN THE FACULTIES?

The autonomy of each faculty, whose administrative council is generally composed of a group of friends chosen by subjective criteria rather than objective standards (except for the student delegate) for fear of shattering the homogeneity of the council, depends upon a number of pressures that determine its activity. It would be interesting to examine the functioning of the "clique" with every faculty. This clique would not formally take action against any of its members, nor contrary to any pressure group. They are an insecure group that does not count upon a stability based on objective criteria of selection and promotion. Instead, they are dependent upon persons rather than upon pre-established standards. As an insecure group, they will not formally make any commitments, and this accounts for the lack of initiative. In many instances, the administrators informally incite the students to request reforms which the administrators themselves do not attempt to bring about because they do not want to be compromised in any way. That is why the life of the University is thwarted and numbed, and its systems favor the anarchy of

41

student pressures within the scale and scope of each faculty, a scale that is fundamental in the University.

ARE THERE EXTERNAL PROBLEMS AFFECTING THE UNIVERSITY?

The rector's authority is quite nominal. He has no vote in the Academic Council or on the Administrative Board. Everything depends on his own personality. If this is not extraordinary, there is considerable danger that the rector's prestige will be utilized by pressure groups to safeguard interests unconnected with the University. The real power of the Administrative Board is reduced to appointing the rector and vetoing the appointments of professors when these are clearly improper.

With this kind of organization, and with the teaching and administrative personnel that it presupposes, we see why it is impossible for the University to really function. A thorough bureaucratic purge, together with proficiency in organization and administrative methods, would be necessary first. Economic assistance should be used to increase the salaries of the principal authorities and the full-time professors as well as the number who are appointed.

CAN "AUTONOMY" WITH REGARD TO UNIVERSITY MATTERS BE CLEARLY DEFINED?

With regard to reforms of the legal statute, it would be necessary to establish and uphold an authentic autonomy, excluding all external influence upon the University. The governing of the University, in view of the selfish orientation of the pressure groups, should be dependent only upon the professors and the students.

The authority of the rector and his secretaries should be

sovereign with regard to executive and administrative matters. The professional and scholastic bodies (deans, professors, and students) should possess only regulative (legislative), consultative, and supervisory powers. This is the only way to ensure the functioning of the University.

Professors should all be chosen by an open, national competitive examination and with the most objective standards and conditions of selection that can be established.

A statute enacted on these bases, along with a reasonable increase in the budget, would permit a high level of teaching and administrative personnel. All the rest will depend on the spirit of service, the technique, and teamwork that imbues those who are able and willing to initiate a really new step forward in the history of our University.

3. A Priest in the University

The personality of a priest, like the person of Christ, is difficult to understand. The mystery of the Incarnation, the presence of the divine within human nature, and the elevation of the human to the supernatural order, produces conflicts in man's mind, which is discursive, and must therefore separate in order to understand. Consequently, in considering one particular aspect, it sometimes forgets others that are no less important.

The priest's mission is, in itself, exclusively supernatural. He must live by divine life and be an instrument for its transmission.

For every high priest chosen from among men is appointed to act on behalf of men in relation to God, to offer gifts and sacrifices for sins. He can deal gently with the ignorant and wayward, since he himself is beset with weakness. Because of this he is bound to offer sacrifices for his own sins as well as for those of the people (Heb. 5, 1–3).

The priest must be in the world, but not of it. He should weep with those who weep, and rejoice with those who rejoice. He must fulfill the incarnation of the Lord, taking upon himself all the responsibility of commitment in the human adventure of his flock.

Although his mission is specifically supernatural, there is also the imperative of charity, for "the charity of Christ impels us." The measure of charity is determined by our neighbor's need. That is why there were bishops possessing the temporal powers of judges and princes. And for the same reason the missionary must practice medicine on many occasions. The law exists for man, and not man for the law.

> You hypocrites! Does not each of you on the sabbath untie his ox or his ass from the manger, and lead it away to water it? And ought not this woman, a daughter of Abraham whom Satan bound for eighteen years, be loosed from this bond on the sabbath day? (Lk. 13, 15–16).

It is for this reason that many priests assume temporal functions, whether in science or in education. But in the field of education, which is a composite domain, their intervention is more easily explained. To be really integral, education must allow an opening towards the supernatural, even though the teaching is limited to a purely temporal field.

A priest in a university can also serve as a professor or an administrator in any of the academic organisms, if his bishop considers it useful in terms of human needs. However, in this temporal activity, even when it is prompted by the imperative of charity, the reputation of the Church is often at stake, whether for good or ill. With regard to motivation no error is possible, because this is a matter of charity. But in the results of this activity, error is indeed possible. Consequently, the priest or chaplain cannot properly make decisions in accordance with a general or comprehensive point of view. He can and must hold fast to attitudes that are in accordance with his conscience, in every case, in the field that is assigned to him. He can also have his own opinions concerning general or comprehensive aspects. Nevertheless, it is his bishop who is responsible for these. And in spite of the human frustrations implicit in subjecting the will to another person, even contrary to one's own judgment, there is great peace and tranquility in knowing that one is thus collaborating in the establishment of the kingdom of God by faith and obedience.

It is sad to see how much difference there is between the judgments of the world and the judgments of God. Among Christians there are no real failures or "blunders," as we say in Colombia. There is a continuous movement of the Holy Spirit through his Church. In this movement, everything culminates in victory, whether failure or triumph, whether approval if received with humility or disapproval if this is accepted with faith.

Recently I received an order from my Archbishop to withdraw from the National University. I was a chaplain there, but quite nominally. Two of my brothers in the priesthood exercise these functions on a full-time basis. I also taught a class in the Faculty of Sociology, and I was a member of the Administrative Council. Since February of this year, at the request of the Archbishop, I am exercising the functions of Dean of the Institute of Social Administration which is connected with the School of Public Administration, an autonomous, official entity, directed by Dr. Guillermo Nannetti. This is a full-time position, whereas my relations with the University were quite occasional or accidental. I have given up these relations. My Archbishop, who has the entire responsibility, felt that I ought to withdraw. He could have compelled me to modify my opinions and activities. But he did not do so, because he knew that I was acting in good faith. He did not want to violate my conscience and I am grateful to him for that. Consequently, on asking me to withdraw for reasons that are not for me to judge, he did so in order to establish his own position in regard to the University problem. He explicitly warned me that he did not want the Church to take the stand which I considered right, because this might be lending the Church to error. Nevertheless, I had already taken this stand myself, and if the Cardinal had supported me, he would have been renouncing the attitude he wished to adopt. I believe that he could do nothing other than he did.

Because of my withdrawal, I have allowed myself to say what

I think regarding the University. Nevertheless, it would be deeply painful to me if any of this were regarded as a banner for temporal struggles. I have wanted to adopt a priestly attitude, but I have run the risk of seeming to be in disagreement with my Archbishop. The best service that could be rendered to me now would be to respect my attitude of obedience which I chose when I decided to become a priest and which I would not accept if it were not an integral part of what I consider to be my mission in the world.

VI.
URBANIZATION AND URBAN REFORM

I would like to go into only a few socio-economic aspects of urbanization and urban reform in Colombia, considering four major points.

1. The Concept of Urbanization

With regard to the concept of urbanization, I believe that although this subject is rather dry and theoretical, it is necessary in order to establish general standards and go forward in a socio-economic analysis. There have been many general concepts of urbanization. Some attempt to describe urbanization as a merely demographic process, that is to say, a concentration of human masses. Others have tried to describe and identify urbanization in terms of industrialization. But these are two different phenomena. Industrialization is certainly a phenomenon which, if not exclusively, is predominantly economic, since it pertains to a form of production and a productive process also. Luis Wirth, an urban sociologist, has given us three criteria in his definition of urbanization: size, density, and functional heterogeneity. As to size, we find a rather large mass of population. Then we must consider the density, which indicates that this large mass of population is concentrated in a rather small geographical area. And finally, there is heterogeneity insofar as this large number of persons gathered together in a small area is widely diversified in functions and activities.

Among these attempts to define the concept of urbanization, we also have the concept of Redfield, who describes urbanization

47

not as a phenomenon isolated from the rest of society, or from the rest of the economic and cultural reality of the country or society in question, but as a continuum or connection between two poles. He defines the two poles very well as ideal poles. For example, ideal rural society does not exist (he prefers to say "folk society" instead), and a total urban society does not exist either, or it exists in a mixture of the two. But there are societies that draw closer to one pole, and some that are nearer the other. Those that are more inclined towards the "folk" pole are usually called "rural," but the word "folk" is preferred because "rural" is exclusively related to an activity or vicinity. On the other hand, Redfield uses the word "folk" in order to give it other cultural and economic meanings which the rural concept does not have. Consequently, "folk" is a type of primitive society, even though we find elements of this primitive society in the cities and the more industrialized areas. We see that some societies greatly approach this ideal type of folk society, while others tend more towards a classical urban type. We hear it said that the concept of economic equilibrium as such does not exist in fact, but is an objective established by economists to indicate tendencies towards this equilibrium or those that depart from it. For the same reason, Redfield expressed the idea of the two poles of folk and urban societies, because in general the definitions of sociologists with regard to urbanization have until now been quite negative in that they ask: What is urban society? What is urbanization?

Urban society is everything that rural society is not. And what is rural society? Everything that urban society is not. Consequently, we find ourselves more or less in both. That is to say, in speaking of large masses of population, these masses must always be related to density, because then the density of peoples, even if they are nomads or completely without any kind of urbanization, can be included in these conceptions if the number of people is what matters. And in referring to density, it would have to be a very large density. But what is density? In relation to what? According to Luis Wirth, the answer would be: in relation to a heterogeneous area. But again, this heterogeneity is related to what? And we are told: in relation to the area in which great heterogeneity exists in its functions. But this is always a very negative definition. Urban is whatever is not rural, and rural is whatever is not urban. That is why Redfield, in a more intelligent manner, establishes the two poles, folk and urban, and between them there is a scale of measurement. Many societies are closer to the folk while others are nearer the urban pole.

Redfield describes the characteristics of each pole which I shall enumerate here. The folk pole is a small society in its functions, generally isolated, illiterate in its culture, with strong group solidarity, a rather coherent culture, with traditional behavior that is spontaneous, unself-critical, and very personal and functional in character. There are no intellectual ends, properly speaking, and the institution of parenthood is of great importance. Consequently, the family is the unit of action. The sacred prevails over the secular. And there is the autonomy of subsistence farming rather than the dependency of a market economy.

Now the urban pole would be the very opposite, as a society with communications in which there is less illiteracy, that is, a society in which there is a formal and developed culture, heterogeneous, with but little group solidarity, an incoherent culture with behavioral patterns that are not traditional but in constant change, formal rather than spontaneous, quite critical and impersonal, with intellectual and rational ends. Parenthood loses its social function, and the family is not the unit of action. The secular prevails over the sacred, and the economy is based on market rather than on subsistence consumption.

If we want to understand fully these criteria in keeping with the classical sociologists, I believe that we should consider primarily those who clearly define these characteristics. They include Weber, Tönnies, Durkheim, and Copley—two Germans, a Frenchman, and a North American.

Weber's concepts of *Gemeinschaft* and *Gesellschaft* are translated as "community" and "society." He says that community is based more upon tradition and sentiment, whereas society is based upon rational ends. In this sense, folk society would be described as community, and urban society would be described as society. This division of *Gemeinschaft* and *Gesellschaft* (community and society) is attributed more often to Tönnies, but this distinction really came from Weber. According to Tönnies, there are societies formed by *Wesenwille* and *Kürwille*. *Wesenwille* defines those formed by a more natural and spontaneous will and *Kürwille* refers to societies formed by a rational and more premeditated will. Accordingly, we could say that folk society is closer to the societies formed by a more spontaneous will, and urban society is fashioned by a more premeditated will.

Durkheim's distinction between mechanical and organic solidarity is also interesting. He tells us that mechanical solidarity derives from functional equality: "We are united because we are farmers." In this case, very few functions are needed, and they are performed by very few persons. On the other hand, organic solidarity requires a complementary system, and that is why it is called "organic," since there are many functions performed by many people, more widely distributed but all of them complementary. Solidarity is thus attained not by homogeneity but by complementary organization, because everyone needs all the others, and each is incomplete. And so we can say that folk society has greater mechanical solidarity, and that the solidarity of urban society is more organic.

With these theoretical and historical concepts affirmed, we believe that we should try to define urbanization. We must first suggest a definition that is quite broad and complex because it is a definition which, frankly speaking, is not yet sufficiently elaborated, in spite of my own attempt to work on this during the past three or four years. And that is why it is so long.

Urbanization is a process which results in the concentration of population masses with considerable division of human activity, and a predominance of tertiary and secondary activities over those that are primary. There is a greater proportion of secondary groups over the primary groups which distribute the money commonly spent for the services.

2. The Process of Urbanization

We shall try to explain all this. In the first place, urbanization is a process. It cannot be conceived as a statistical matter, but rather as something that is taking shape. With regard to the concentration of large masses of people, there is already the element of density, and here can be perceived what we consider to be both evident and essential in the creation of cities, namely, the broad division of human activity. With socio-economic progress new necessities are created, and in view of these new necessities people must become specialized because they cannot undertake individually all the activity to supply these new necessities. With specialization they become more technical and also more open to progress and efficiency. This explains why they must live near one another so that there can be a complementary division of labor. And consequently, they go on creating cities in order to obtain the maximum benefit from this division of labor and, from the geographical point of view, be near one another and advance together.

We said, moreover, that the tertiary activities, that is the services, are predominant. These include commerce, administration, education, transportation, and the personal services. Then there are the secondary activities, comprising the processes of transformation, sometimes characterized as manufacture or industry. As we said before, one associates "industry" with "urbanization" and yet most typical of urban society is the tertiary sector, not the secondary, because there are isolated industries and industrial nuclei that are not cities, more especially in the Soviet Union and the United States. To be truly a city, there must be the essential and formal element which is tertiary activity, that is to say the services of commerce, education, and everything else that service implies.

When we speak of "predominance," we are using the word in a relative or proportional sense, because sometimes there is also primary activity in the city. We cannot say that agriculture, mining, hunting, and fishing are totally excluded in many cities, because agriculture includes the small, domestic orchards and vegetable gardens that are not very significant economically, but are much more so than we sometimes suppose and are also important because of the social activity of the persons involved.

We spoke of primary activities, total predominance, absorption, and tertiary and secondary activities as related to those that are primary. We also mentioned the greater proportion of the secondary groups as compared with primary groups. The former are based upon formal relations, more concerned with a person's occupation than with the person himself. In a small town or village, we may hear someone say: "I'm going to ask Tom to send a telegram." Everyone knows that Tom is the telegrapher and everybody's friend, who smokes a cigarette with you when you call on him and invites you to drink a glass of beer on Saturday. Tom is an institution, and he is the telegrapher. But in the big city, nobody mentions the telegrapher's name because the relations are very superficial and transitory. The primary groups are those in which the relations are much more intense, more frequent and intimate; they are "face to face" relations, as we say. The family is a primary group. Recreational and neighborhood groups are primary. But the labor unions, professional associations, and corporations are secondary groups which establish relations that are much more superficial, based far more on a person's occupation than upon the person himself.

We know, of course, that there are some secondary groups in the big city in relation to the primary groups. Moreover, they are united by an economic factor. It is important that we give some thought to the partition of the common services. As you know, it is much easier to have one aqueduct for a million persons than ten aqueducts for one hundred thousand persons. It is more economical, because if the basic expenditures are divided among a larger number of people there is greater economy, and the volume of economy will be governed by what the economists call the law of increasing returns. While an enterprise, or in this case a city, is growing, the common costs are divided among an ever larger number of people. That is why the large cities are economical.

But there comes a time when industry expands as rapidly as the city, resulting in counter-production which begins to lower the profit returns. The same thing happens from the social point of view. When the city becomes very large, the law of diminishing returns begins to make concentration less economical. Obviously, this depends on the region, the city, the administration, and many other factors, and consequently we cannot establish a general norm as to what size is best for a city. What must be undertaken in every particular circumstance is a special analysis of the economy, resources, transportation facilities, administration, and so forth, in order to learn how much a city should grow if it is to remain economical.

With regard to the process of urbanization, if we accept the division of human activity as the essential variable, after neutralizing the other variables, we can say that urbanization began when the first nomadic people (if it really did begin with nomadism, which is not yet completely proven, but we can assume this in order to fashion a descriptive and graphic form) became sedentary, thus initiating the process of urbanization. For that was the beginning of the division of labor between those who wandered with herds of cattle or those who were engaged in hunting and fishing, and those who were farming the land. In any case, the principal source of sedentary life was agricultural activity which required permanence in one place.

Later, the activity of labor developed a little more with the advent of manufacturing for persons whose sedentary existence was located in a particular place. They needed clothing, shoes, tools, and this was the beginning of the industry of consumption which, of course, led to the tertiary activities of commerce, transportation, and administration. These, in turn, began to be divided.

In each of these primary, secondary, and tertiary activities we find subdivisions, and insofar as a person only knew how to make shoes, for instance, this created a need to find someone to

53

farm the land for him, or make clothes, or give him an education. It was because of this division of labor that the creation of cities with their large concentrations of people was begun. That is why I believe it is not coincidental that in earlier times there were no large cities. All the ancient cities like Memphis, Thebes, and even Athens were relatively small in relation to the population in general, because naturally the division of labor is both cause and effect of socio-economic development.

With this socio-economic development there is a very large increase of the urban population. I found a percentage census of population in cities of more than 100,000 inhabitants. Unfortunately, however, it was published in 1950, and I could not find one that was more recent, covering the whole world. It shows that 13% of the world's population is found in cities of more than 100,000 inhabitants: in North America 29%, Oceania 41%, Europe 21%, the Soviet Union 18%, South America 18%, Central America and the Caribbean countries 12%, Asia 8%, and in Africa 6%.

The rural population of Colombia was estimated at 60% in 1951 and today, according to Dr. Machado, it comprises more or less 53%, with an urban population of 47%. However, we must consider these statistics from the sociological point of view, with certain reservations, because this report considers an "urban center" as any town with more than 5,000 inhabitants. Nevertheless, from the sociological point of view, and with regard to "folk society," there are cities much larger than 5,000 people whose activities are entirely rural, living completely off the produce of the land, including regional capitals such as one which I recently visited, Lorica, which can be called a totally rural town or area where everyone lives off the land and anything else is purely accessory. And because we cannot wholly adhere to these statistics, we believe that in Colombia the information concerning the ten cities of over 100,000 inhabitants is far more revealing. This shows us that there are about two and a half million people, or 30% of our population, who have urban customs, which is more important than the size of the population. It seems to me that judging only according to size is not sufficient, from the sociological point of view.

What factor really determines this urban growth? It is not the birth rate, which is much lower in the cities than in the country, and at times there is a natural decrease, that is a decline of the population from the point of view of natural growth, compensating the birth rate with mortality. Consequently, the big factor of urban development is migration from the country to the city. In Bogotá we find that 60% of the inhabitants were born elsewhere. Thus it is now most important to know and examine the factors of migration. These include expulsion from the country to the city and the influence of the city's attraction upon country people. With regard to both, we believe that the economic, social, and political factors should be considered, since this phenomenon of migration from the country to the city is so important for urbanization.

We shall first consider the economic factors that underlie expulsion from the country. They can be divided into those phenomena concerning property ownership and those which pertain to income. With regard to property ownership, we know that the immense majority of the Colombian population is composed of small landholders or those who own no property at all. Now property is not flexible. We can increase the dimensions of an industrial enterprise, adding to the number of machines and installations, but we cannot increase a piece of land. The most we can do is to fertilize and mechanize it, but this can only go so far, because these technological processes are always limited by the extent of the land itself. For small landholders, subdividing the land among their sons implies a division of poverty, as I have already pointed out. If a family owns ten acres, and gives one acre to each of their sons, this already makes it impossible to earn a living, and if each of these had ten sons, there would only be a tenth of an acre for each of the latter. We see that the problem of land with regard to ownership results in the migration of people who leave the rural areas to seek something other than land ownership.

With reference to income, we know that it must come from ownership or from the day wages of those who do not possess any land. And with regard to land ownership, we see that the yield from agriculture is very low because of poor methods of cultivation, the lack of intelligent planning, and the fact that agriculture is often attempted on steep slopes while cattle-grazing is permitted on lands more suitable for agriculture. Moreover, as we shall see later, the farmers do not possess a truly agricultural market, but quite simply a narrow subsistence consumption, because they can find no one to buy their products for lack of transportation and the lack of careful planning that would result in sufficient productivity at lower costs. These are the economic factors which cause the small landholders to live in really wretched conditions.

As for income based on day wages, we know that they are lower in country areas than the real wages in the cities. Many people argue that the cost of living is lower in the country and that although farm workers in fact receive lower wages, their living expenses are also lower than in the cities. But the cost of living is lower only with regard to agricultural products which generally are not the things that they buy, or which are purchased on a minor scale. These must be exchanged for manufactured products, including clothing of all kinds and many household articles, trucking and shipping arrangements, and all the other purchases apart from food, which come from the city at higher prices than in the city itself. Real wages must be distinguished from nominal wages or gross income, and in relation to the cost of living, real wages are much lower in the country than in the city. This is still another reason why people are driven from the rural areas; they are fully aware that city wages are higher. This is a social factor, but the fact that in reality these city wages are much higher is also an economic factor producing migration from country to city.

From the social point of view, among the social factors of expulsion from the country areas are the lack of public services in hygiene, education, transportation, administration, and in recreation also, which is of great importance because of the monotony of country life. An underdeveloped country is much less able than other countries to extend these services, which will not be shared by many people.

The lack of opportunities in country areas, where there is so little social mobility, and the homogeneity in activities make the lifelong country-dweller believe that he has but little chance to improve his situation, even if he is mistaken about this. It reveals a psychological and sociological barrier in regard to social progress. Another aspect is the feeling of inferiority. Generally, the country-dweller feels inferior to the city-dweller. The person who has traveled to the city, or studied in the city, or has relatives and friends there, is esteemed as someone of greater importance and worth. Consequently, a feeling of inferiority can impel the country-dweller to move to the city.

Furthermore, in very small societies with cultural patterns that are more or less traditional and sentimental, there is a rather irrational and very rigid social control. This is the kind of control exercised by the family over an individual member, or by the neighborhood over any person, making him adjust to very narrow norms which he has not personally assimilated. These norms include the religious standards; if he does not go to Mass, the whole neighborhood knows it. If he gets drunk, everyone hears about it. Escape from this social control may thus be another reason for the country-dweller's move to the city.

From the political point of view, there is a greater number of opportunities, a greater chance for participation in political and governmental affairs, and more information concerning national events in the urban area. Moreover, the factor of violence must be mentioned here; often the country-dweller leaves his rural home to seek security in the city.

With regard to land ownership, possession itself is not very important. There are many ways of life and forms of prestige that are not closely connected with property or rental income or tenancy. Today, the holding of stocks and bonds, which are a form of participation in commerce and industry and a much more flexible kind of property ownership, and even the mere fact of possession, whether of land or of other kinds of property, is not so important or so necessary in the cities, as the Pope pointed out in the encyclical *Mater et Magistra*. The concept of property has now greatly evolved, and for many persons it is more important to have a good education than to own land or other property.

There are also a few factors of social security which draw country-dwellers to the city. We have reference to security from the educational and legal points of view, because contracts are better fulfilled, and government loans together with family allowances, grants, and subsidies are more frequently available in the cities. The system of economic inducements and incentives is also attractive. From an economic point of view, the individual would sometimes rather have the security of a retirement income than a small parcel of land which he must divide among his sons. And investment finds much greater productivity in industrialization. We must admit that the productivity of capital, when utilized in industrial and urban investments, is greater than agricultural productivity.

We should mention again the fact that more economical and more numerous services as well as greater and more diversified opportunities are to be found in the cities. There is a certain urban mirage which is a purely social factor, apparent in the city's attraction and fascination affecting the rest of the nation. While this mirage is a phenomenon to be found in developed countries, it is even more obvious in underdeveloped countries, where there is a sharper contrast between the feudal or sometimes even pre-feudal system found in many rural areas and the totally modern system which we noted in the cities of Colombia and other Latin American countries.

The lure of freedom is another important factor. Ever since the Middle Ages there has been a traditional belief that there is more personal freedom in the city than in the country, because there are fewer social controls. This belief alone brings people to the city, where they can lose themselves among the anonymous masses and, as Dr. Machado has said, if they associate with others, it is in groups or associations which have been formed on the basis of need or desire rather than custom, and whose membership is voluntary rather than imposed. There are, of course, certain environmental and social impositions in the city too, but the pressure of such impositions is much less intense here than in the country. For example, in the political perspective, we noted the greater possibilities of participation, and fewer impositions by leaders and others, which are social aspects politically applied.

3. Urbanization and Development

Now to proceed with the third section, which concerns the way in which urbanization is related to development. When we examined Redfield's description, which we rounded out with the opinions of other sociologists concerning folk society, it seemed as though what was being referred to was an underdeveloped society. Development as such has greater reference to structures than to indicators. In general, however, development has been presented to us in terms of indicators concerning literacy, capitalization, population growth, mortality, and a whole series of other factors that are merely symptoms externally manifesting something more profound which is the structure itself.

We know that West Germany after the war showed signs of being an underdeveloped country. There was very little capitalization, no industry, and a whole series of signs and indicators of underdevelopment. But we cannot really say that Germany was an underdeveloped country after the war, because it possessed the structures of a fully developed country. Therefore I believe that it would be interesting to analyze briefly the structures of development, but I would want to analyze them in relation to urbanization, or rather in relation to those structures of underdevelopment that can influence urbanization or be influenced by it.

In the first place, we must consider the structure of values, for this is generally very important with regard to many of our problems, including agrarian reform and economic planning. People never realize that they must take into account the problem of values held by others concerning these matters. I am convinced that the rise of a mystique of development is one of the great things that happened in Cuba, the Soviet Union, Puerto Rico, and the Philippines. What does it mean when we say that a country possesses the mystique of development? It means that social values have changed, whether by revolution of the Communist type, or by a nationalist revolution, as in Egypt or even in the Soviet Union, where it is considerably nationalistic. The most important factor in these revolutions, we feel, is that they produce a change in the structure of values. Wherever there was no mystique of development, it soon originated among the population. All the media of propaganda and all the programs of the government are adapted to this national mystique. The same can be said about the mystique of agrarian reform. When there is agrarian reform without a mystique, it is very difficult to apply planning of any kind. This is important for development and sometimes is a by-product of development itself. Consequently, planning is sometimes very artificial in our countries because it is attempted by a succession of experts who have studied abroad and who are not understood by people of inferior levels. But even if some people understand them, nobody pays any attention to their ideas because the people believe that these are simply the follies and nonsense of young economists. Accordingly, as long as there is no mystique for planning which begins with the primary school and extends to all levels, and so long as values are not revolutionized, planning cannot be applied.

As Christians we are not supporters of the unhealthy structures created by capitalism, and we must take note that the standard of efficiency and productivity, if human and Christian criteria are sacrificed, then becomes harmful, as has happened in capitalism. Nevertheless, this standard is a positive element without which no progress is possible.

In this matter of productivity and efficiency we must learn the secret of producing things more conveniently, more pleasantly, and more simply. We must develop a kind of individualism that is highly purified and dedicated, in order to seek efficiency and finally surpass capitalism in whatever is both efficient and productive, not from the individual point of view but rather in the social perspective.

There is also the concept of evaluation, closely connected with productivity and planning, that must likewise be related to values which nobody in our country wants to evaluate. Essentially, this is the sentiment of "self-criticism" as it is called by the Marxists, but which is something which Christians have practiced since the origin of the Church as personal self-criticism, which we call an "examination of conscience" and which must be applied to all institutions and activities. It is also one of the tests of development.

The standard of "welfare" and "social security" is also indispensable for development, for this requires that majorities rather than minorities be taken into account, and that not merely the material necessities alone be considered, but man in his integral and social dimensions. With regard to institutional structures, we know that they are more or less a reflection of the structure of values, including institutions which must be well-organized, institutions which should be efficient and functional, and others which must be evaluated and corrected. Finally, these are institutions that ought to regard and respect man as an end, and not merely as an instrument.

However, as I see things now, the question of industrialization cannot be sufficiently covered by seminal themes, and so I want to go a little further into this matter. In the economic structure it is important that we advance from the level of subsistence farming to the structuring of a market. We must move forward from one-crop exportation to diversified exports and finally attain to industrialization. Without these three things, I believe that economic development is impossible. To establish a market economy there must be an effective demand for production. One of the things most emphasized by Professor Currie, which was not sufficiently taken into account by those who were not economists, was that a merely potential demand for a product is unimportant. We hear that in our country a great deal more can be produced from the agricultural point of view, because all of this will be consumed. And why? Because the Colombian people are ill-fed, as we learn from the studies of the F.A.O. and the statistics concerning the consumption of proteins. And of course all of this is very true. However, the economists are not saying that there is no hunger, but that when all is said and done there is a lack of money. In other words, the potential demand exists, but there is no *effective demand*. And to create effective demand it must come either from other country-dwellers or from the urban centers or from abroad.

The other country-dwellers who can make effective demand are generally those living in other climates, because the rest can produce for themselves. Now if other country-dwellers are to make this demand, something is needed for the producers. There must be productivity at lower cost together with transportation and a planned marketing system. But this does not exist at present. Furthermore, there must also be purchasing power on the part of the other country-dwellers who, in turn, need a marketing system, general planning, and low production costs so that they can sell their own products, and a vicious circle is thus established!

We do not believe that effective demand can result from other country-dwellers; it can only come from the urban centers. But then what is needed? There must at least be transportation facilities, because if people have money they can buy things even if the prices are high. But what really happens? They do not have the money to spend, because our industrialization is insufficient. Therefore, if we are only going to favor migration, without a parallel industrialization, we will merely be creating an urban proletariat which will not be able to consume the rural products.

In the matter of foreign trade, we must accept the fact that we cannot export our agricultural products, because there really is no competitive market. This means that we cannot enter into competition in the international market. There is much talk about market shortages, suggesting that we find out what is lacking in the international market, or what has not reached the saturation point, and we hear considerable talk about meat and livestock of all kinds. However, there is no serious attempt to discover shortages in supply, but only the possibility of competition. Competition in the cattle market seems to be quite problematical because of the technological methods used in production, and even though there are shortages in supply, we would have to sell at such low prices that probably, if our cattle-raising is not based upon certain techniques, we could not compete in the cattle market at all. Consequently, we must seek those markets in which we can be competitors, especially with regard to agricultural and tropical products that are produced technologically, thus lowering the prices.

If we consider the question of manufactured products, we must find out what the city-dwellers will buy. But if we do not raise the purchasing power of the working class, we will not be able to find any market among city-dwellers at all. Farmers know that if there are no big investments and no technology in agriculture, they will not have any purchasing power either. Competition is even more difficult in foreign trade. I believe that except for countries less industrialized than our own, it will be immensely difficult for us to develop a competitive market for manufactured products unless we can finally enter into a Latin American common market, but in my opinion, this is still a dream and will remain so for a very long time.

What then are the essential conditions in creating a market economy? We believe there are two: investments and technology. Any government investment policy established should be centered upon the necessary infrastructure, including transportation, irrigation, the search for electric energy, and so forth. Investments are also needed for mechanization, and these would be largely private investments, although unfortunately, as we know, capital is either exported abroad or used for unproductive and luxury articles, and this is one of the most serious problems in an underdeveloped country. Consequently, it is very important that we succeed in channeling investments towards productive enterprise and also towards long-term credit with favorable conditions.

With regard to technology, we see that there must be a technological advance for agriculture and for urban dwellers also. I feel that these are the two great deficiencies of Operation Colombia, especially since it claims that the policy of investments in the urban areas can be carried out by simple decision, almost as though we were living under a dictatorship and there were no pressure groups to hinder or impede all of this. We are assured of a great many investments of a public nature and that there are many factors to consider. We must not, of our own free will, concentrate investments in housing projects at the start, as was said, so that we may now develop the consumption industries which give purchasing power to the immigrants who work in them. But I believe that there has been great deficiency in the investment policy and in the technological training and acculturation of the rural immigrants. A simple transfer of rural immigrants to the city is not enough to ensure this acculturation and technological advance. If our agrarian reform can result in producing farmers who possess a managerial and technological mentality and an intelligent approach to efficiency, evaluation, and social welfare, then we will successfully attain a stage preparatory to the concentration of cities with more rational bases.

With regard to agricultural technology, the attempt to hasten the adoption of technical methods and the intensification of agriculture by legal decision is also quite utopian. The important thing is to proceed with a practical agricultural technology that results in the abandonment of marginal lands and gradually leads to concentration upon the more productive agricultural areas.

When we consider industrialization, we must not forget that there can be no real development without it, because in the first place industrialization stimulates the remuneration of our national labor force, and this remuneration is higher than the primary sector receives and even higher than the earnings of the tertiary sector in underdeveloped countries. As a result, if the work force of our secondary sector receives higher pay and the national income is more widely shared, we will be paying our own workers rather than North American and other foreign workers through purchase of all the manufactured products. Moreover, the productivity of industrial ventures is much greater than the productivity of agricultural enterprises. That is why there can be no real development without industrialization.

In view of these factors, in what way does industrialization contribute to development? With regard to the structure of our values, we saw that a primacy of the national criterion prevails far more than sentimental and traditional standards in urban society. Next, there is the criterion of technological productivity which is much more easily developed in an urban society than in a rural society. The diversification of occupations also produces much greater competition in the city because of the proximity of competitive groups. The fast pace so evident to us when we arrive in a big city is simply due to the environment. The person who does not compete or even try to compete does not survive.

Professor Currie presents a problem concerning the structure of the economy which can only be solved by urbanization. He mentions the fact that the major consumers of farm products are city-dwellers. And as long as we have a great many rural producers who are not consumers, agricultural production will have no outlet. He goes on to say that the only way to create consumers who are not producers, and who will be the source of effective demand, is by industrializing the urban inhabitants. These are irrefutable observations. But another question arises: How can this be done? Can it be accomplished in two years, as he suggests?

We often hear it said that with foresight we will not fall into the error of creating large urban concentrations. This would be easy in a country that is already urbanized and industrialized, where the rate of urbanization is gradually diminishing. In the United States, for instance, we can readily find factories far removed from the urban areas and there are industrial centers which are easily accessible because of transportation facilities. The complementary aspect of occupations no longer requires geographical proximity because both human and material communications have been facilitated by technology, but it is very difficult for us to really succeed in accomplishing industrialization without urbanization. We believe that our economy of resources in general, and the allotment of the services and their costs, require for the present that we think in terms of urbanization. It is like thinking about Operation Colombia without a previous agrarian reform. We cannot leap over certain stages, because this would entail such vast investments that we would no longer be underdeveloped if it were possible to finance them. This means that we would be undertaking an operation which implies full development in order to emerge from our underdevelopment!

With regard to the social structure we believe that urbanization will be the system that creates a middle class which will ultimately bring about our process of development. The official limit and goal of this process is the creation of a cultural, political, and economic middle class. And what is the reason for this effort? That there is no powerful middle class means that the national income is now badly distributed. But will urbanization create a middle class? Urbanization based upon careful planning and the controlling of markets, of investments, and therefore of employment opportunities will ensure a larger income for persons living in the city and, consequently, more income for those who live in the country, because they will then be able to sell to the people who want the products of the farm. Gradually, all of them will climb to higher economic levels. We know that in the underdeveloped countries the cultural factor is very dependent upon the economic factor, which means that there could be more schools built and a general spreading of culture. From the administrative viewpoint, we know that cultural and economic factors are very influential, and with the gradual increase of urban values there will also be an increase of the values of development. Moreover, the social structure will likewise be transformed if we achieve a more rational urbanization.

4. Urban Reform

To accomplish this urbanization efficiently, we need an urban reform, and this must not be considered merely as a matter of housing, with the aim being to enable everyone to own his own home, any more than adequate agrarian reform can be conceived simply as a plan that will enable everyone to own a parcel of land. Essentially, urban reform consists in planning urbanization on technical, social, and human bases together with a policy of investment. Agrarian reform can be helpful in part because it would give greater economic capacity to persons acquiring new land. Unfortunately, we do not possess any coercive instruments efficient enough to ensure the investment of capital within our own country in the first place, and in the second place to channel it into productive enterprise. The possession of such instruments would greatly facilitate industrial development in the urban areas. However, although we do not have these instruments, investments in the urban areas in general are more alluring than in country regions, because of the city's attraction, which is felt not only by the country folk who have moved to the city but by the landholders also. Consequently, it is possible that this will enable us to establish an investment policy in the cities which would control investments by taxation and by certain laws channeling them into heavy industry rather than into the manufacture of consumer goods. Furthermore, urban reform requires a serious consideration of technological training for our workers. This entails a greater effort, but we know that we still lack techniques. We have an unskilled labor force that absorbs most of the wages, thus making the situation more difficult for persons who migrate from the country to the city. On the other hand, our skilled workers are in short supply. In 1954, for the normal industrial development then under way, we needed 12,000 more skilled workers annually, but industrial training was only producing 1,000. Now at last in SENA they are successfully producing about 5– 6,000 skilled workers, which is a gigantic and very effective effort, but it still leaves us with an accumulated shortage of 50%.

It is clearly apparent that in order to effect an urban reform conceived in this way, there is an urgent need for technological training of our workers. This should follow, as Dr. Machado has pointed out, a planned investment policy, including certain measures against profiteering by speculation. This is the dreadful phenomenon of our cities and one of the rigid factors in the housing market. In the process of urbanization, speculation involves the land itself, where construction will be undertaken. This land that is reserved for construction is in great demand. Consequently, it is much more productive, according to the law of supply and demand, to let the land surrounding the cities become a source of quick profit rather than make it socially useful, as Dr. Machado pointed out. And then what happens? If there is no official intervention, people will continue to get rich on the sale of this land, raising the cost of housing not only in these particular areas but everywhere else as well. Urbanization is also hindered because speculation fosters the mushrooming of squatter slums. We know that when the normal channels and processes of development are not open to people, they resort to abnormal activities to seize what they want. If urbanization and urban extension are not carefully planned, squatters do not pay for the land but simply seize it, and slums are soon created. Now all these invasions could be remedied by strictly limiting the cost of land so that it could be urbanized normally. At present it is the inflexibility of the land market that exercises some degree of control, but control ought to be exercised by governmental action, as was done in connection with social welfare in keeping with a "standard of equity," as the National Constitution affirms. By this standard of equity, the government can expropriate land, even without indemnification. From the Christian standpoint, we note that in this case, pertaining as it does to the common good which expropriation requires, even if no one is indemnified, it can be done.

In conclusion, I would simply like to annotate four points. The first indicates that we cannot separate urbanism from socio-economic development. We must accomplish the urbanization of our country. Second, if this urbanism is to become the line of development, it must be coordinated with a policy controlling investment, with a technological training of our labor force, and with a policy concerning urbanized land. To achieve this, we need an economic urban reform. And the investment policy should not be oriented exclusively towards the urban problem, but encompass all of our national investments. Third, an educational policy with regard to the matter of technology is indispensable. And fourth, we will need an effective legal policy which, unfortunately, like agrarian reform, will be subject to many pressure groups if we are not able, as Christians, as young people, and as university students, to create other pressure groups that favor a reform aiming at the welfare of our society.

VII.
THE PROBLEMS OF RURAL SOCIETY

1. Variables Common to Every Rural Society

OCCUPATIONAL PATTERNS

Cultivation of the land and cattle-raising are practically the only activity of the Colombian peasant. In general, all other rural work is wholly conditioned by this factor, including marketing, religious and domestic activity, and so forth.

Violence created necessities for country-dwellers, and together with these it required a division of labor and specialization. For activists, in addition to the needs required in any warlike action, the specific needs of guerrilla warfare soon became apparent. These include espionage, clandestine communications, the supply of provisions, social assistance, public relations, and other necessities.

With regard to passive groups we should also note the appearance of new necessities, including vigilance and collaboration among themselves and with guerrilla bands, along with all the needs imposed in the case of forced migrations.

For each of these necessities, it was indispensable to detach individuals from the rural community to perform the necessary tasks habitually. This resulted in a kind of specialization which, although rudimentary, is important with regard to social relations. These relations in rural society, as a consequence of the lack of division and specialization of labor, are characteristically more intimate, frequent, and personal.

This kind of social relationship leads to a type of folk society so well described by Redfield. He defined it as a small, isolated, illiterate, and homogeneous society, with a strong feeling of solidarity. The way of life is conventionalized within a coherent system which we call a "culture." Behavior is traditional, spontaneous, uncritical, and personal. There is no legislation, no experimentation, nor any reflection for intellectual purposes or goals. Parenthood and its relations and institutions are largely empirical, and the family group is the unit of action. The sacred prevails over the secular. And the economy is based on mere subsistence rather than on a market. (Cf. Robert Redfield, "The Folk Society," in *The American Journal of Sociology*, 52 [January 1947], 293.) All of these characteristics were exactly applicable to our rural society before the surge of violence.

Among these characteristics we should mention traditional spontaneous behavior, uncritical and personal, as an effect of the preponderance of primary relations over secondary relations. Now the lack of division of labor and of specialization contributes to this predominance, since the *person* who performs many functions is the real basis of social interaction much more than is the function itself. The lack of specialization explains why there is no social requirement or social expectation with regard to progress through formal instruction.

Group solidarity is another effect of the lack of division of labor, if we have reference to the mechanical solidarity in Durkheim's theory. (Cf. E. Durkheim, *De la division du Travail Social* [1902], XXXII.) This mechanical solidarity naturally produces a coherent system of life based on tradition and sentiment.

In the theory of Tönnies, our rural society is much closer to his concept of community (*Gemeinschaft*) than to the notion of society (*Gesellschaft*). On the other hand, the economy of subsistence stimulates primary relations much more than the secondary and is one of the causes of the inadequate division of labor. The effects of these factors on the prevailing attitude towards social change are of great importance. The predominance of primary relations over the secondary begins to disappear through division of labor, greater specialization, and consequently the multiplication and diversification of social functions.

71

In communities affected by violence, social interactions begin to be based more upon the functions performed than upon the person himself. Group solidarity becomes more organic than mechanical, that is, based more upon the complementary aspect of the various functions than upon their homogeneity. Social relations begin to be based more on reason than on tradition and sentiment. Behavior ceases to be traditional and spontaneous, and becomes critical and impersonal.

SOCIAL ISOLATION

Among the variables common to all rural societies we find social isolation, an element included in Redfield's concept of folk society. This ecological phenomenon is due to the low demographic density and the absence of communications that characterize rural societies. In underdeveloped countries social isolation is aggravated by the lack of transportation and the absence of communications of all kinds. In Colombia, particularly, isolation is even greater. The Colombian population is concentrated in the mountainous zone and in the valleys separated by mountains. Rural neighborhoods and settlements are isolated not only from the big cities but also from the administrative municipalities and other country towns.

Violence increased rural migrations to the city and also between the various rural localities. The armed forces, in addition to their own systems of communication, were a human conduit for the transmission of news, social values, and behavioral patterns established between the city and the country, and between the various rural districts.

As a result, rural populations have entered into contact and are now aware of common needs. They are acquiring a group solidarity by confronting the knowledge of their socio-economic reality together with knowledge of other and higher standards of living both in the country and in the city. Local cultural patterns are becoming more widespread and a phenomenon of assimilation of these factors is occurring, thus beginning the process of gestation of a rural subculture in Colombia. With regard to social change, the fact of having created a group solidarity which Marx would call "class consciousness," means that Colombian peasants are beginning to constitute a pressure group at the bottom of the social pyramid. This can be a pressure group which, by good organization, will become important in the transformation of the social, political, and economic structures of Colombia.

THE IMPORTANCE OF RURAL NEIGHBORHOODS IN SOCIAL LIFE

Because of the isolation just described, it is to be expected that the "neighborhood" is of major importance in the social life of the rural community. Human activity in this society has a direct reference to geographic localization. The lack of any division of labor almost completely excludes the necessity of displacement to another district. Consequently, the neighborhood, together with the family, develops the most efficacious institution of social control in rural society. The neighborhood's sanctions of approbation or condemnation have great influence upon the behavior of the peasant.

We know that there is a close connection between the power of social control and the standardization of behavioral patterns. Factors of anonymity rarely appear in an isolated society exercising strong control. In a community of this kind there is but little capacity of assimilation among individuals, because in order to live in society they need only adapt themselves mechanically to the traditional patterns of behavior. This explains the coherence of folk society which Redfield mentioned. And it also explains the lack of experimentation and of reflection for intellectual ends. Behavior is more spontaneous than reflective, and that is why the assimilative capacity is inconsiderable.

Violence breaks the very framework of the rural neighborhood.

The guerrilla bands become new controlling elements that are more regional than local in scope. Official pressure is manifested, quite often for the first time in rural areas, exercising pressures of all kinds, from physical violence to economic allurements on a regional scale. The possibility, and sometimes the necessity, of migrating often liberates rural groups from the social control of the neighborhood community. The groups of reference for social control grow in number. In addition to the family there are guerrilla bands, and along with the neighborhood itself there are groups of harassed peasants who are more or less belligerent. The military army, and the civilian militia composed of urban groups, intervene in the violence and consequently in the rural communities. All of these groups, with their different behavioral patterns and values, relax social control, as occurs similarly in the cities. The peasant, accustomed to acting without reflection and uncritically, conformably with fixed standards and patterns, loses every behavioral norm and becomes readily adaptive, as far as possible, to the various groups of reference. This anomalous behavior becomes generalized among the conglomerate country masses as an effect of the shattered social isolation of the rural neighborhood. The rural communities that have endured the factor of violence are now wide open to any kind of cultural contact. The breaking of its social isolation has made the rural neighborhood lose importance in the social life of the country-dweller, and it has established new institutions, both regional and national in scope, which characterize the new subculture originated by violence.

In a way similar to that which occurred with regard to social isolation, a relaxation of local social control takes place in rural areas through the increase of controls that are independent of geographical location. This multiplication of various controls can be explained by the diversification of activities among rural inhabitants. However, this diversification does not arise from some factor of development of economic productivity, but should be attributed to activities of destruction, defense, or simply subsistence, which are hard to fit into a plan of socio-economic development for the nation. In this case, it should also be noted that we encounter sociological phenomena of urbanization without the concomitant factors of industrialization or the creation of cities.

The new organisms of control and the relaxing of them have resulted in more reflective and more critical behavior, but in accordance with a scale of values that is completely pathological.

INDIVIDUALISM

Isolation generally produces cliques and closed societies. However, when the isolated labor of each individual is combined with this general isolation, individualism then arises as a logical consequence. This is what happens in rural societies of small landholding structure or engaged in the stationary occupation of harvesting the crops. Interests are then individual, and collaboration occurs only in terms of these interests. Certain associations and institutions composed of these individuals are quite transitory in character and do not contradict but rather confirm individualistic behavior insofar as the latter is understood as the resultant of the pursuit of objectives in terms of predominantly personal interests. Individualism is an attitude defined by its motivation. However, social behavior is an indication of the motivation of individuals, and sometimes it is the only one known or which can be known.

In view of the predominance of the small landholders and the harvest hands among the rural population in Colombia, we can be sure that an individualistic attitude is quite generalized, especially in the more isolated areas. The collective habits and customs of certain indigenous communities have been abandoned by the great majority of our Colombian peasants.

Violence, however, largely shatters rural individualism. Government officials introduce behavioral systems that make teamwork indispensable. Similarly, the government has organized "peace guerrillas" to combat bandits. The guerrilla forces, both formally and informally, constitute elements of collective effort that greatly weaken the individualist outlook of our rural inhabitant. Organizing norms for guerrilla forces are now being established in which collective interests take precedence over individual interests. Informally, the guerrilla bands had to work together as a team to carry out their tasks in connection with both their warlike activities and subsistence. Groups like that of El Pato were organized, and by their collective efforts a sugar mill was built, a vegetable garden was seeded, various projects were undertaken that benefited both farmers and ranchers, along with sowing, weeding, and harvesting the crops. The group solidarity typical of every marginal community, and especially any group considered to be outside the law, is fully verified within the guerrilla bands.

Among country-dwellers violence creates circumstances that compel them to break away from their individualism. Mass migrations, the defense of rural communities, organization for production, and so forth, create attitudes of cooperation, initiative, and awareness concerning common needs. If we add the creation of a rural subculture and class consciousness to this shattering of individualism, we have a new social situation in the Colombian rural community. This means that such a community constitutes a social element possessing internal cohesion, initiative, and dynamism when confronting the possibilities of social change.

CONFLICT WITH "OUTSIDERS"

The rural groups described in terms of the preceding characteristics are necessarily of the closed type, with "a strong feeling of solidarity," according to Redfield's description. This is an internal solidarity which is generally in direct relation to the degree of conflict with "outsiders" of all kinds.

In fact, in our rural communities there is an attitude of distrust with regard to institutions, leaders, and everyone in general who does not belong to their social group. These "outsider" institutions can be classified as governmental, ecclesiastical, and private. But it should be noted that many of these governmental, ecclesiastical, and private institutions belonged to the rural group itself in the sense that they were identified with the rural community to a much greater extent than with the government, the Church, or any other entity at the national level. The use of the first person plural in referring to "our" church, "our" courthouse, or even when speaking of certain ranches or herds of cattle, reveals this feeling of solidarity with institutions closely identified with the community. However, this rural attitude towards official institutions above and beyond the municipal level was not an attitude of overt conflict but rather a kind of cautious reserve and distrust. This also applies to ecclesiastical and private entities that are not connected with the locality.

Nevertheless, it is indispensable to distinguish two types of rural communities that are very different. One is the small town or village, and the other is the rural settlement or neighborhood. Before the rise of violence, a policy of accommodation existed between these two types, subordinating the local neighborhoods and rural settlements to the town or village communities. This accommodation, however, sometimes changed into conflict, especially for political reasons. These political motivations were possibly a symbol manifesting a latent conflict occasioned by a situation of settlement or neighborhood inferiority with regard to the administrative municipality of the district.

Among the different rural communities we have noted a competitive relationship that occasionally degenerates into conflict, but this is not often violent. Nevertheless, we sometimes find a policy of accommodation between one rural settlement and another. And their common conflict with the administrative municipality results in a decrease of tensions and the creation of solidarity among them.

With the coming of violence, human relations in our rural society were fundamentally transformed. The official, ecclesiastical, and civil institutions, even if local in character, were often considered as "outsider" institutions, thus preventing their assimilation with the rural population. And although relations with these same institutions at the regional or national level caused overt conflict that was often violent, a relation of conflict was established with such institutions at the local level also.

Accommodation with the government, the Church, or the landlords was destroyed. This same relation of accommodation between the rural population and the town was also changed. Some of the townsfolk formed an alliance with the official, ecclesiastical, and civil institutions that were in conflict with the peasants, while others sided with the latter. Some elements of the "town" then entered into cooperation with elements of the settlement, and some with the "outsider" institutions.

Relations between rural neighborhoods have passed through various phases. The mild and superficial conflicts that preceded the rise of violence were acutely sharpened, acquiring a distinctly political aspect at the start. The peasant populace formed groups under the symbols of the traditional parties, Liberal and Conservative, in an attitude of violent conflict. The Communist groups arose as a third element, occasionally as a country group that did not want conflict with other country-dwellers, but only with the authorities, whether official or not.

The first effect of violence was to divide the rural populace. But when the state of violence became chronic, an important factor of social change became apparent. As the violent pressure of "outsider" groups diminished and socio-economic necessities increased, a new kind of solidarity among Liberals, Conservatives, and Communists was created. This occurred, for example, in the Valle del Cunday early in 1961.

This new kind of solidarity is more organic than mechanical, more rational than sentimental, blotting out not only the political divisions accentuated by violence, but the divisions existing between rural groups before this new factor appeared.

With regard to the leaders, before the rise of violence there was in rural societies a concentration of leadership in the "town" or administrative municipality. The bureaucratic, traditional, and charismatic leaders could always be found there. But some of them could be found in the country settlements and neighborhoods, although these men had very little influence upon official decisions in governing the rural community at the municipal level, reserving for themselves merely a small quota of power among the peasants of a particular locality. (This classification of leaders was defined by Max Weber.)

The structure of this rural leadership changed with the introduction of violence. The charismatic leaders of the country settlements acquired an importance that was often greater than that of the leaders living in the "town" or administrative municipality. The traditional or civilian leaders of the town who adhered to the institutions that favored and fostered adverse violence lost their status of leadership among the rural populace. The same thing happened to the charismatic leaders who, therefore, were no longer charismatic leaders in the strict meaning of the term.

Quite logically, in the electoral processes a new type of leadership arose in the rural settlements. Political officials necessarily had to establish agreements with these new leaders in order to obtain the collaboration of the rural masses in their plans and programs.

With regard to other individuals among the "outsider" groups, we should note that the feeling of solidarity or distrust concerning them was closely connected with their attitudes in times of violence. As a matter of fact, however, many of the "outsiders," including those of the upper class or of urban origin, were accepted into the peasant ranks always and whenever they manifested real solidarity in the armed struggle. And many genuinely rural elements were rejected if they showed any solidarity with the adversaries in this same struggle. Solidarity with individuals was based more on common interests than on ecological origins, and far more on rational motives than on those which are traditional.

The conflict with "outsider" groups and the restructuring of social relations in rural communities fundamentally changed the whole structure of our rural population. It created a new type of rural solidarity that is more rational and is the basis of a conflict with the "outsider" groups that do not identify themselves with the interests of these communities.

2. Characteristic Variables
of Rural Society in Colombia

POLITICAL SECTARIANISM

What is ordinarily called "political sectarianism" is a form of group aggression and, concretely, a group that is part of an organization which exercises—or claims to exercise—governmental power. In addition to the element of aggression, we should include the correlative notions of intergroup security and insecurity for those who are excluded.

All adherence to a group is both an effect and a cause of the individual's need for social security. This factor of security provided by the group is more intensive according as the insecurity of being outside the group is even greater. In the developed countries, of course, there are institutions that guarantee social security in ways and forms that are independent of group membership. Consequently, the need to belong to a group is considerably less in these countries than in ours. Moreover, as social aggression is greater in an underdeveloped country because frustrations are generally more numerous and more intense, we may conclude that political sectarianism is a by-product of the lack of socio-economic development.

In the unindustrialized countries the small minority holding power, as we noted before, constitutes a self-contained group which possesses the greatest amount of security within the society. The only way to lose their security would be by a change of structures resulting in their loss of social control. Obviously, this kind of change could only originate in the excluded group comprising the vast majority of the population who are unable to make the upward climb. The very fact of being a ruling minority constitutes an element of insecurity whenever there is discontent among the majority. Consequently, some mechanism is necessary to satisfy the majority, maintain the structures, and, if possible, make any change of these structures highly dangerous.

A political party can accomplish all these things whenever it complies with certain requirements. In the first place, it must satisfy the majority of the populace to some extent, and these satisfactions must be sufficient to avoid discontent. In the second place, it must relate the satisfaction of needs to the maintenance of the structures, and in the third place, it should create systems to make structural change really dangerous.

A political party in Colombia is an instrument for the satisfaction of certain needs of the majority of Colombians. And because of the bureaucratic pork barrel in an underdeveloped country, where skilled workers are few in number and a high percentage of the national income is applied to administration with but few technical demands on the latter, the political party is an important source of social subsistence and of social expectations of subsistence for many Colombians, since the distribution of pork barrel funds, jobs, and privileges is dependent upon the party. In other words, many of our citizens live by public employment. But many more depend upon public jobs, even though they do not have them, by their hope or prospect of getting such jobs. Therefore, many Colombians are directly or indirectly dependent upon the political party.

However, if this dependence is also to imply a guarantee of maintaining the socio-economic structures, there must then be a required dependence upon the ruling class. For this reason, if the party is to be a capable instrument of conservation for this class, it must be structured fundamentally on the correlation and connection of all social needs with the ruling class. As is logical, if this correlation does not produce technical or rational advantages and benefits, it becomes necessary to seek sentimental motivations to justify it. This accounts for the traditional or sentimental basis of the party systems, although the bureaucratic pork barrel, which in fact is distributed by the ruling class, could be administered by the majority of the population in a more technical and rational way.

The maintenance of the structures can only be solid and lasting if its disruption entails danger for the class that does not derive benefit from the system in force. Political sectarianism is the instrument whereby the ruling class succeeds in making the majority find an intergroup security proportionate to the insecurity of those who are excluded.

In brief, the political party has functions to perform with regard to both the ruling class and the majority of those who are governed. For the ruling class, it constitutes an element for the conservation of structures by partisan sentimentalism and by political sectarianism. It does not permit a restructuring of parties on rational bases which would transform the structures by introducing a government by majorities.

For the governed class, the social environment of insecurity produced by political sectarianism makes the party a group providing refuge together with the unique ability of establishing relations with the ruling class, the fount and source of their own security. This relationship must be established with the indispensable condition of conformity and compliance with regard to the political party in question. Conformity of this kind implies demonstrations and guarantees primarily by sectarian manifestations against the opposing party. Political sectarianism is, therefore, a two-edged sword which reinforces the conformity of the governed class and ensures the stability of structures for the ruling class.

Violence broke loose as an instrument of sectarianism in order to better serve the purposes which we have attributed to the latter. That is why violence did not occur between the ruling classes but only among the peasant populace sentimentally divided between the traditional parties and suffering from greater social insecurity, which bound them still more to these parties. Consequently, as soon as a political union of the ruling classes was achieved, violence continued in order to ensure the necessary sectarianism which prevents the restructuring of the parties with rational bases capable of transforming the structures.

With a policy of this kind, it is to be expected that any individual who dares to dissent from the directives of the traditional parties will be considered as marginal or almost as an outlaw. The appearance of "watchdog" societies is symptomatic, because they are composed of members of the ruling class representing both political parties. The formal purpose of these societies is to harass Communists. More informally, they ostracize any dissenting individual or anti-conformist movement that appears on the political, social, or economic scene. Violence, therefore, does not favor or protect one or the other political party in particular. Sometimes it gives its support to a minority party, leveling by terror the political forces that were not leveled by electoral processes. However, violence fundamentally protects and favors the whole ruling class, regardless of their adherence to one party or the other.

In spite of all this, violence unchains a social process unforeseen by the ruling classes. It has awakened the consciousness of the peasant, giving him group solidarity and a feeling of superiority and security in action. It has opened up possibilities of social ascent and institutionalized aggression. In consequence, Colombian peasants are beginning to prefer the common interests of rural society rather than the interests of a political party. This will have the effect of constituting a social, economic, and political pressure group capable of changing the structures in ways that are the least foreseen and least desired by the ruling class. It is very possible that, due to violence, political sectarianism will be changed into class sectarianism, which has already occurred in many rural areas in Colombia.

THE LACK OF CLASS CONSCIOUSNESS

If we enter into a discussion concerning the definition of a social class, we will be neglecting the real purposes of our analysis. For our own objectives it should be sufficient to use a definition that is widely accepted. When we speak of the "peasant class," we are referring to a certain social group whose economic status is the lowest in our Colombian society. Dedicated to an occupation within the primary sector of production, this group is predominantly localized in the rural areas of the country. Class consciousness is something that prevails with respect to a series of existing social relations within the group just defined. These relations imply the exclusion of outsiders. When this class consciousness is combined with initiative and organization in and for common action, the group which possesses it is capable of influencing governmental decisions and, therefore, it can become a pressure group. In many underdeveloped countries, the peasants have been organized in various ways. Agrarian movements in Latin America, for example, have had an importance that contrasts with their significance in our country.

The more pronounced character of the variables already mentioned, especially individualism and isolation, has resulted in a lack of class consciousness among Colombian peasants. Furthermore, the cultural isolation of our country together with the outdated and obsolete technical equipment of our communication systems, have hindered the cultural interactions that are necessary for a social change capable of creating an authentic class consciousness. The absence of contacts has produced an inadequate awareness concerning our own needs, for lack of knowledge of other groups of reference. The lack of ascendant social mobility has resulted in the institutionalizing of fatalism with respect to a few necessities about which there is some awareness among the peasants. But even if by some circumstance or other there is an awareness of such necessities, and fatalism has been replaced by an attitude of initiative in activity, this has generally occurred at the level of the individual. Conflicts with peasant "outsider" groups have hindered the creation of rural solidarity. And political sectarianism has acutely aggravated the disunity.

Even after the rise of violence, we can observe certain rural communities which did not experience its influx or influence, either directly or indirectly. In these communities we find a delineation of their awareness concerning necessities, fatalism with regard to progress, and a lack of collective security among the peasants.

We have considered the effects of violence in the creation of class consciousness among Colombian peasants, and we can now sum up our analysis of the changes brought about by other variables. The excessive importance of the local neighborhood, isolation, individualism, conflicts within the groups and with "outsiders," the feeling of inferiority, the absence of any social mobility that is vertical and ascendant, together with latent aggression, imply a general lack of class consciousness. By altering the variables previously mentioned, violence begins to create a class consciousness. It generalizes the social relations among peasants of nearly the whole country and makes everyone aware that these relations pertain exclusively to the peasantry. Moreover, it produces solidarity for action beginning with informal influence upon governmental decisions; and by means of political agreements it begins to influence the established structures. From the lack of this class consciousness as a point of departure, the peasants are now becoming a pressure group that will ultimately be decisive in the social transformation of Colombian structures.

RESPECT FOR PRIVATE PROPERTY

From the various reports and accounts of the Indian chronicles, historians of the colony, and the Latin American historians, we can conclude that the most widespread form of property ownership in the indigenous communities was a collective possession of land.

The colonizing procedure of the Spaniards did not fundamentally affect the native mentality concerning property. Rural collective systems continued under new ecclesiastical, military, or civilian masters.

The emancipation movement introduced liberal ideas, among which was the notion of private property as the base of the political and social structure in Colombia. Respect for private property gradually became part of the patrimony of Colombian cultural values. Before the rise of violence, our peasant populace held fast to a formal respect for private property, but informally this respect was occasionally disregarded or repudiated in practice. During times of violence, the concept and system of the *jus primi possidentis* was introduced.

Expropriation of land at the lowest price, invasions, control of the harvests and marketing procedures, carried out by the guerrilla groups, led to the loss of this cultural value which had been acquired by our peasants during the last century. In communities where this factor arose, there were land invasions organized so easily that they cannot be explained in terms of economic pressure alone, but were based upon the practice, during a period of violence, of utilizing the property of others for immediate subsistence purposes.

Although this effect of violence is accessory and apparently limited to certain times and places, it is salient with regard to social change. If, as we noted before, the peasant populace is now being constituted as a pressure group, it is important to know the cultural patterns of this group. And if respect for private property is no longer an element among these patterns and standards, it is quite possible that in the change of structures which may be accomplished by the pressure of this group the whole structure of property and ownership will be directly attacked.

3. Conclusion

Based upon the preceding analysis, we can say that for Colombia violence has constituted the most important socio-cultural change in our rural areas since the Spanish Conquest. It was by their recourse to violence that our rural communities were integrated, in the process of urbanization in the sociological sense, with all the elements which this implies, including the division of labor, specialization, socio-cultural contact, socialization, an outlook and acceptance of change, the awakening of social expectations, and the utilization of methods of action to facilitate social mobility by channels that were not foreseen by the structures in force. Violence, moreover, established the necessary systems for structuring a rural subculture, a peasant class, and a pressure group, revolutionary in character, constituted by this same class. However, violence has brought about these changes through pathological procedures and without any correspondence with the process of economic development of the country.

Although it is very difficult to predict, it is quite probable that there will be structural changes, adequately far-reaching, and accomplished by the sole initiative of the present ruling class in order to enlist all these anomalous forces in a process of development that is technically planned. Moreover, the orientation towards agrarian problems which has characterized the most recent government administrations could produce the effect of creating a basic leadership capable of channeling peasant pressures towards objectives of social and economic development. If these pressures are exerted in a sufficiently skillful and energetic manner, they could change the structure of our ruling class, provided that this class is able to evaluate in time the danger of a transformation which might destroy it completely, if it is unable to adapt itself to inevitable social change.

VIII.
THE BIDIMENSIONAL MAN

In a pluralistic society with economic and social problems, should a Christian simply go on waiting or should he begin to act if he finds himself overwhelmed by perplexity?

There are two objective realities. One is the reality of the natural and the other is the supernatural. There are objective supernatural realities which we perceive by faith. Objective symbols of the supernatural include miracles and sacraments. All through sacred Scripture we find that water is the visible sign of purification, and in the New Testament it is the sign of conversion and the obtaining of eternal life. Natural realities are attained by reason and supernatural realities are attained by faith.

But is it really possible to separate the natural from the supernatural? Can a Christian, possessing supernatural life and grace, exploit his fellow workers at the natural level? Can he condone dishonest political interventions?

We can know completely natural realities by observation and reason. We can know a man by observation when we see, hear, or touch him, because this is concrete, individual knowledge, sensory rather than intellectual. This is abstraction in the first degree. And then we can abstract certain elements concerning him: How big is he? How much does he weigh? How old is he? This becomes an abstraction in the second degree, even a mathematical abstraction. Still further, we can abstract the essence of the man, an abstraction in the third degree.

There are, therefore, three degrees or stages in acquiring knowledge: observation, reasoning, and universal abstraction. The latter will not vary even though the data obtained in the first two stages of knowledge may be different. If there is any variation, it means that they were not authentic, or more probably because the search for these data was not carried far enough.

With regard to a man's essence, which is a universal and ultimate abstraction, it does not matter whether the men we observe are young or old, tall or short, handsome or ugly, yellow, white, or black. An abstraction in the first degree reveals the scientific laws which give us the constants of the observable realities that exist or occur among beings and are attained through systematic observation. Logical reasoning can then follow, and in turn this will enable us to reach a generalization that gives us physical certainty which will not be altered by individual changes. Consequently, our philosophy can be immutable and adaptable to our faith. A Christian philosophy can be defined as one which arrives at universal principles that are not contrary to revealed truth.

In this field we can therefore possess a community of ideas with all men, whether Christian or not, who share this same philosophy with us. When we accept universal philosophical principles that are not obtained through faith, we enter into communion with non-Christians, materialists, atheistic idealists (Hegelian), and pantheists, among many others. Quite obviously, if there is a natural reality different from supernatural reality, then knowledge of the natural, reached through observation, reasoning, and generalization, is not specifically in the possession of Christians, but is common to all men, for example, at the level of scientific laws, and thus our achievement of solidarity with the greater part of mankind becomes much easier.

The social sciences are no longer merely speculative, but are beginning to be positive. They have abandoned universals in order to become inductive. Their point of departure is systematic observation which enables them to attain to a logical generalization of constants. As an example, any human group involved in conflict becomes much more united in spite of its respective variables at the economic, cultural, and other levels. Now the social sciences are acquiring the status of positive sciences, adhering entirely to the field of observation and experimentation.

And if we take action based upon irrefutable facts (which only a lunatic could deny), we will enter into community and agreement with most of mankind, whether Christian or not.

In conclusion then, as Christians we may affirm once again that in our knowledge of natural realities, we can and must be in agreement with an immense part of mankind.

There are distinct kinds of knowledge, both natural and supernatural. Man was created in the image and likeness of God. In the design of God, man should be supernatural, but if man is not so because he lacks grace, he has a supernatural vocation nevertheless. Man's nature has been raised to supernature, and therefore man is able to act supernaturally. But the supernatural is not superimposed upon man like a hat. It is united substantially with the natural. This unity exists in man, in Christ, and in God. Our use of natural things implies supernatural acts if we are raised to the dignity of sons of God. For Christians, everything is supernatural. Our action results in supernatural acts; we do not supernaturalize things.

A Christian, receiving grace and living supernaturally, is meritorious, even if in keeping with his abilities and opportunities he does not attain to very full knowledge or very solid truth. But for the non-Christian this is not so, because even if his knowledge is more valid, his life is not meritorious because he lacks the supernatural life. The non-Christian physician, for example, can be a better physician than one who is Christian. The same can be said of the philosopher, the chemist, and the artist.

Integrated reality consists in making the supernatural of itself convey greater efficacy than the natural. In natural matters, however, in being natural, the Christian as Christian is not more efficacious. In science, politics, and economics, the discoveries of non-Christians can be more efficacious than the findings of Christians.

Man is an integrated reality, naturally and supernaturally. How can we distinguish those who act supernaturally or those who possess grace? We cannot say that all who fill the churches, going to Mass and Communion every Sunday, necessarily possess grace. Love is the indication or sign justifying our presumption that they possess grace.

The Christian loves, and this love distinguishes and defines him. External practices serve as a means for attaining love, and they should in turn be motivated by love. Such practices without love have no validity. The non-Christian who loves and is seeking in good faith possesses grace. He is laboring supernaturally and is a son of God. On the other hand, the Christian who carries out the external practices without love is not Christian. The integrated man, from the material and spiritual standpoint, and in the natural and supernatural perspective, should be someone who loves.

In view of these things, what should a Christian perceive in the natural? With regard to all that is natural and temporal, Christians are not different from others. But we have an obligation to be better and thus differentiate ourselves. Love is our moral imperative, and if it is real, it ought to be integrally efficacious, both in the natural and the supernatural sense. If we are not efficacious, if our lives produce no fruit (for by this we shall be known), we are not loving. Consequently, the temporal commitment of the Christian is a mandate of love. He must strive efficaciously to become an integral man materially and spiritually, naturally and supernaturally. In the natural sphere the Christian is distinguished by his way of loving in the manner and through the impulse of Christ. "Greater love has no man than that he lay down his life for his friends." If the Christian seeks this greater love, he will attain to the greatest efficacy in all things, whether speculative or positive.

Through the levels already mentioned, we are in agreement with non-Christians. But only if they love can we know whether they stand with us or not, and as Christians we must go on loving to such an extent that we become more and more closely united with mankind.

IX.
HOW PRESSURE GROUPS
INFLUENCE THE GOVERNMENT

A pressure group is composed of individuals who together determine the decisions of national policy. They are a specialized society, but pressure groups do not necessarily exercise power in a formal manner. There can be functionaries and bureaucrats in public positions who belong to these groups and exercise power officially in the interests of the pressure groups.

Consequently, real power is vested in groups of this kind. This real power will be democratic in character if the pressure groups represent majorities, and will be oligarchical when these same groups represent minorities. In Colombia, access to form part of the pressure groups is controlled by a small minority that constitutes the only real pressure group, because the really important decisions to maintain effective structures are dependent upon this group. And this small minority pressure group, by means of economic power and the requirement of conformity, controls the other powers, whether cultural, political, bureaucratic, military, or ecclesiastical.

The concentration of economic power in Colombia is obvious. Statistics concerning the bad distribution of our national income and per capita income, the deplorable division of land tenure, and so forth, are widely known. To gain access to cultural power, one must first possess economic power, because of the structure of our educational institutions.

The upward climb into the ranks of the political hierarchies requires conformity with those financially powerful and a cultural minimum as well. Bureaucratic power also requires this minimum and even greater conformity, because the upward ascent through bureaucratic channels in Colombia depends upon the judgment and decision of the bureaucratic higher-ups, and these men cannot maintain their own public status if they are not in conformity and agreement with those who hold economic power.

Military power in our country can only be justified as the defender and upholder of enforced structures and, in the final analysis, of the economic power. The latter repays or compensates the military men with financial, social, or even political privileges, as circumstances may require. These correspond to their conformity with the "established order."

The ecclesiastical power in our country is united to the financial and political powers because they possess interests in common. The conformity of ecclesiastics lends support ensuring the maintenance of these interests.

The popular classes, comprising the large majorities, do not constitute pressure groups because they do not possess awareness of their common needs, nor are they united in their activity. They have no organization that is national in scope, nor even a minimum of common political objectives. If the majorities fail to obtain these requisites, Colombia will never become a real democracy.

X.
SCIENCE AND THE DIALOGUE

During one of the most significant periods of the Cold War, a conference was held in Geneva to determine systems for the control of armaments and nuclear forces. At this conference the American and Soviet scientists reached an agreement. Controversy arose when an attempt was made to specify the policy that should be adopted in the use of controls over those who had established the agreement.

The positive sciences, whose conclusions can be verified by positive observation, are an instrument of union and dialogue between persons of different ideologies.

The social sciences, until the end of the last century, had been considered as speculative and normative sciences. They were not to provide abstract principles, universal and metaphysical definitions, or any value judgments for concrete action. It was claimed that all the social sciences should utilize absolute categories, and that they should define absolute truths concerning society and declare what was good or bad in politics, economics, administration, social assistance, and so forth. Absolute theories concerning society flooded literature at the end of the last and beginning of the present century. It was the high point of social philosophy. Comte and Marx were the two classical exponents of this movement.

Nevertheless, during this same period certain positive scientists began to appear within the social disciplines. They became aware that society was an objective reality that could be examined without recourse to value judgments or metaphysical abstractions. Many of these scientists embraced positivism, which is a philosophical position. As often happens, the discovery of the usefulness and worth of the positive and whatever was empirically observable quite dazzled the discoverers, and they began to insist on generalizations. They would only admit what could be verified by the senses. In the face of this gratuitous generalization there was a reaction, if not of opposition, at least of much distrust in the positive social sciences.

Those whose cultural conditioning imbued them with high respect for the speculative values felt that they had been personally injured. In this kind of cultural environment, as for instance among the Latin peoples, the positive sciences were regarded with suspicion, and for this reason, among others, they were neglected. The positive focusing of the social sciences was simply suppressed in extreme reaction.

In Colombia, we resented this reaction profoundly. Culturally, the speculative and normative values hold a very high place. This explains the flowering of philosophers, political leaders, and moralists among our intelligentsia. It was a necessary and constructive flowering, but inadequate for integral progress that is both spiritual and material.

The social scientists who were trying to undertake positive analyses of social reality gradually abandoned their positive philosophical positions, for the affirmation of the empirical did not imply a denial of the speculative. At this time the non-positive scientists whose ideologies were speculative found entry into the domain of positive social science. A different ideology did not hinder exact agreement in the observation and analysis of the same reality. Nevertheless, empirical objectivity does require a particular intellectual and temperamental approach.

An approach of this kind is very difficult to acquire except by slow process together with a university discipline oriented in this way. It is an approach that does not seek to deprive anyone of his particular beliefs or his value judgments. And it must also prevent any deformation of the objective analysis by these beliefs and judgments.

In Colombia, members of the teaching profession who stress this focusing on objectivity in the social sciences are quite new in the field. Graduates within this discipline are still few and far between.

However, the popular masses, especially in foreign countries, who have contributed to positive social science, have not been wholly alien to those who have traditionally been concerned about social problems in our country, including political leaders, lawyers, and moralists. These men have made the laborious effort of learning foreign languages, thus making up for whatever was lacking in the supply of translations or original books in Spanish. If they did not always translate a whole book, they at least translated complete passages, even from German, with the purpose of understanding new orientations and explaining these to their fellow citizens who do not possess the same linguistic facilities. But this is not enough. It is very difficult to become autodidactic in those disciplines in which there is need not only for knowledge but also for a different approach and mental discipline.

With regard to certain analyses that do not claim to be philosophical or normative, our autodidactic scientists always react by demanding "that the author declare himself." They say that he should not limit himself to analyzing and expounding. He should say whether something is good or bad, and whether it is in accordance with metaphysical truths or not. This requirement shows that it is not enough to have done some reading in order to change a mental attitude. Books are inadequate. What is needed is a process, a discipline, and an intellectual approach.

It is clearly apparent that defining a situation or describing a reality is insufficient to solve a problem. But it is no less certain that nothing will be seriously solved without objective knowledge of the problem's fundamental elements. And this is precisely the groundwork of the sociologist.

Politics and philosophy divide the modern world into antagonistic and radical forces. Social problems and their solutions are the source and root of the conflict. Why do they not seek a point of contact and vehicle of dialogue in objective and scientific analyses of reality? Only the enemies of sincere dialogue are opposed to these positive scientific disciplines. They are enemies of dialogue because of their ignorance and their desire to preserve their privileges. They do not want to lose control over those who are trying to develop a science that does not depend on the traditional categories, even though it does not threaten their position either.

If realistic discoveries are made, is this not helping political leaders, moralists, and others to find better solutions in agreement with everyone's ideology? After all, what difference does it make whether reality is discovered by a farmer, a politician, a military man, or a priest? Positive reality can be discovered by individuals regardless of occupational or ideological differences. And if something is discovered which can be verified by experiment and inquiry, should it be kept secret simply because people are not accustomed to the presentation of discoveries until value judgments are added to them?

It is certain that truth gives us freedom. "The truth shall make you free," as Jesus said. And the freedom of certain social theories, if wholly submitted, can seem dangerous to those who are in power. We must let our priests, military men, lawyers, and any citizen try to analyze our society. We should enter into discussion with them concerning the truth of these analyses. And both politics and morality should be based upon study rather than intuition.

Judgment of intentions should be left to God, and we should utilize all the approaches and discoveries which will lead us to truth. The distinction between positive and normative sciences is precisely what prompts us to demand that all ideologies be scientific, joined together around the empirical verifications that no one can deny or reject. This union centered around the positive is the beginning of a dialogue that does not imply further or factional divisions. It does not presuppose any victors or vanquished. It can be a source of peace.

XI.
TWO SUBCULTURES

A country's lack of real leaders is all the more apparent when the problems confronting society are especially massive and complex. These problems are so obvious that they cannot be avoided, and because of their complexity they unmask the ineptitude of the political leaders, not merely in their attempts to solve them, but even in their efforts to discuss them.

The recent verbal display of our political leaders and our newspapers was a sad spectacle of incontinence, unrealistic outlook, ignorance and, therefore, irresponsibility. The elusive will-o'-the-wisp of tropical eloquence brings to mind, within a different cultural setting, those decadent courts of the Renaissance Era, when national leaders and representatives spent their time participating in amateur plays, charades, and pantomimes while the people struggled in wretched poverty. When these leaders finally awoke from their irresponsible degeneracy, they found themselves facing the gallows.

The verbal battle in our country has centered around three topics, discussed in the superficial manner of a decadent class. They touch upon violence, pressure groups, and structural changes. It is not possible today to require a politician to be a specialist. But neither should he be allowed to discuss any subjects with total intellectual irresponsibility. At the very least he ought to be required to consult an expert, or a book, or at any rate a dictionary!

1. A Complex Symptom

Violence is a very complex symptom. Sociologists, psychologists, and criminologists have examined it from different perspectives, and have done scholarly research that is scientifically valuable. Violence is the complex symptom of a social situation that can only be explained in terms of many factors. But our political leaders try to cope with it, both in theory and in practice, with excessive simplicity. There is groundless dogmatizing about it. And when some study or essay appears which, although not perfect, at least tries to be scientific, it is judged from the standpoint of sentimental and anachronistic political traditions. When there is talk about "pressure groups," not even a dictionary of sociology is consulted. The real meaning of the term is not known. It is simply taken to be a Marxist expression or a combat slogan. And it is only to defend or attack pressure groups that they are mentioned at all, but never to analyze or improve them.

The "structures of reform" are not specified or defined. This term is now entering into demagogical jargon like the word "oligarchy" or the expression proclaiming "moral restoration of the Republic." Since neither the ends nor the means are specified precisely, our political discussions continue whirling around unscientific verbalism that is lacking in seriousness and realism.

2. The Two Subcultures

How shall we explain the irresponsible attitude of those who have the obligation to resolve problems that can no longer be postponed?

It is possible that in Colombia there are two incipient subcultures that are gradually becoming more independent, dissimilar, and antagonistic. One of these subcultures derives from an educated class, those having an annual per capita income of over three thousand (U.S.) dollars. Their buying habits can be defined in terms of industrial consumption. They represent approximately fifteen percent of our population. The other class, more or less illiterate and having rural customs, possesses an archaic subculture. They constitute the remaining eighty-five percent of the population in Colombia. Each has its own system of values, behavior, and attitudes, which are now becoming antagonistic. Whatever communication there is between these two classes is breaking down.

3. Different Meanings

The same expressions have different meanings for each class. The following list is hypothetical, but it could be verified and demonstrated by direct research.

Expressions	For the Upper Class	For the Lower Class
Oligarchy	Insult	Privilege
Violence	Banditry	Non-conformity
Pressure groups	Chosen caste	Exploiters
Revolution	Immoral subversion	Constructive change
Change of structures	Revolution	Fundamental changes
Agrarian reform	Illegal expropriation	Acquisition of land by the poor
Political parties	Democratic political groups	Oligarchies
Social sensibility	Popular attitude	Paternalism
The press	Fourth estate	News monopoly
Black Hand	Center of Studies and Social Action	A sinister secret society
Trade unions	Conflicts between classes	Vindication
Communal action	"Peaceful" solution	Local organization
Left	Subversion	Non-conformity
Communism	Crime	Revolution
Capitalism	Economic system	Exploitation
Imperialism	Marxist slogan	"Gringo" influence
Fidel Castro	Communist leader	Revolutionary chief
Devaluation	Economic measure	Poverty
National Front	Political unity	Union of oligarchies
Alliance for Progress	North American aid	Imperialism
Church	Institution for preservation of order	Reactionary force

Army	Utilizable force	Violence
Bureaucracy	Administration	Parasites of the State
Parliament	Democracy	Parasites of the people
Pacification	Repression of delin-quents	Death of guerrilla fighters
Peace Corps	Voluntary altruists	Tourists or spies

This list is highly arbitrary and could continue interminably. However, it shows how class values can be polarized. Moreover, the systems of communication between the two classes become ever more precarious, because the absence of common expressions make dialogue impossible, and the lack of dialogue engenders incomprehension. When a cultural barrier of this kind arises, simple common sense is not sufficient to overcome it. Real contacts must be made in order to re-establish a dialogue. There can be contacts of all kinds, and among the principal means of affectuating them are participation, observation, and scientific research. Unfortunately, however, neither the one nor the other of the two classes is able to utilize these methods, because for the lower class there is a lack of access to the upper classes and inadequate education, while the upper class is hindered by isolation and by its superficial analyses. This isolation is conscious or unconscious. Even those who travel around the country for political, technical, or other reasons, are received by the local circle of higher-ups, which isolates them from any possible contact with the spokesmen of the lower class. Nevertheless, the popular class in Colombia has been steadily renouncing mere talk and is now interested only in deeds. Some political leaders are aware of this and in their campaigns refer to their past achievements. But the electoral abstention in recent elections reveals the scepticism of many Colombians.

4. A United Front

As long as our popular leaders do not fashion a united front which discards the personalism that arouses so much suspicion among the people, and if leftist chatter, which is almost as stupid as the babbling of the ruling class, is not soon ended, the popular class will no longer keep in step.

Only deeds and facts will abolish this lower class and reconstitute it as a majority pressure group. It will be a group exerting pressure through action, and will reveal to our present leaders all that they could not grasp or achieve for lack of realism, skill, responsibility, and above all for lack of dialogue. Through pressure they will compel the ruling class to make real contact with the people and enlist the collaboration of scholars who are trying to make a scientific study of the attitudes, values, terminology, and institutions of the lower class.

This contact and collaboration are indispensable prerequisites for acquiring an awareness of the difference in lingual expressions and general culture, and for overcoming this difference. A common lingual terminology can thus be established as an irreplaceable basis for solving the problems of the majorities by those minorities that now hold the responsibility of power.

XII.
THE CHRISTIAN APOSTOLATE
AND ECONOMIC PROGRAMMING

1. The Essence of the Christian Apostolate

To determine the essence of the Christian apostolate we must precisely determine two aspects: the ontological and the epistemological. In other words, we must define what is meant by the Christian apostolate and how we can recognize it.

WHAT IS THE CHRISTIAN APOSTOLATE?

Christ is the apostle par excellence. If we define the essence of his mission, we will be defining the essence of the Christian apostolate. The Christian apostolate is an activity whose purpose is to establish and extend the kingdom of God.

God endowed Christ with power "in order that to all whom thou hast given to him he may give everlasting life" (Jn. 17, 2). In the Gospel of John, we find that the words "life" and "eternal life" are used in the same sense as Matthew speaks of the "kingdom of God" and as Paul refers to "justice" (Alfred Durand, *L'Evangile selon Saint Jean, Verbum Salutis* [Paris, 1927], p. 77). This identification, moreover, is quite legitimate, since the kingdom of God consists in possessing this life itself. Christ came that the sheep of his fold "may have life, and have it more abundantly" (Jn. 10, 10). Consequently, the essence of the apostolate is to labor in order that all men may have supernatural life and have it abundantly.

HOW CAN WE RECOGNIZE THE
CHRISTIAN APOSTOLATE?

Apostolic work consists of everything that leads others to possess supernatural life. This work is always efficacious, even if its results are not visible. The ultimate and essential result is invisible because it consists of supernatural life itself. There are, however, various indications of the existence of supernatural life which condition apostolic activity. It is important that apostolic activity be guided and directed so that it will produce these indications as means rather than as ends. There is an external factor which is both an indispensable indication and a condition of apostolic activity: the manifestation of love for one's neighbor. If this manifestation is inspired by supernatural life, in addition to being an indication and condition *sine qua non,* it becomes an end and purpose of apostolic activity. We shall explain this statement when we clarify other indications of the existence of supernatural life and therefore the proper means of the Christian apostolate.

The ordinary means to obtain supernatural life are foretold in sacred Scripture and in the practice of the Church: prayer, the sacraments, and the Mass. However, the utilization of these means, although a good sign of the existence of supernatural life, does not give absolute certainly of this existence without a special revelation (Denz. 805). These means can be used in practice without charity, and if there is no charity, they are not signs of supernatural life.

Profession of faith in God and in Jesus Christ can also indicate the possession of supernatural life. "Now this is everlasting life, that they may know thee, the only true God, and him whom thou hast sent, Jesus Christ" (Jn. 17, 3). Nevertheless, one can hold and profess the faith without possessing this supernatural life: "and if I have all faith so as to remove mountains, yet do not have charity, I am nothing" (1 Cor. 13, 2). If a Christian does not have charity, it serves no purpose for him to manifest all the signs of possessing supernatural life. But if he has charity, he has everything, "for he who loves his neighbor has fulfilled the law" (Rom. 13, 8). Love, therefore, "is the fulfillment of the law" (Rom. 13, 10).

We cannot have supernatural life without charity, and our charity must be efficacious. Charity is essentially supernatural life. But if we are to have real charity, real love must necessarily exist in our hearts. The good works we do to help our neighbor are indispensable if this love is to be authentic. Therefore, inefficacious charity is not charity at all. "By their fruits you will know them" (Mt. 7, 16). "And if a brother or a sister be naked and in want of daily food, and one of you say to them, 'Go in peace, be warmed and filled,' yet you do not give them what is necessary for the body, what does it profit?" (Jas. 2, 15–16). God's judgment on men is fundamentally based on the efficacy of our charity. In the final judgment (Mt. 25, 31 ff.) our eternal destiny will be determined according as we have given food, drink, lodging, clothing, refuge, and welcome to our brothers.

In conclusion, we can say with certainty that there is no supernatural life in persons who have the faculty of reason, if good works in helping our neighbor are lacking. These works, both material and spiritual, are not in themselves absolutely certain signs of the existence of supernatural life. There can be other good works that are not supernatural. To become supernatural, they must necessarily be performed by someone in the state of grace, and this requires that the person have the faith, even if it is only implicit. Anyone who acts in good faith can be saved. It is not certain that outside the Church there can be no grace, or that the only way to belong to the Church is through formal reception of the sacraments. There can be a baptism of desire and a penance of desire. Therefore, supernatural life can exist even without explicit faith or any formal reception of sacraments. On the other hand, there can be no supernatural life in rational individuals if no good works are performed to help our neighbor.

This is not a problem of exclusion, but rather of priorities concerning policies and procedures in apostolic action. In a word, it is a problem of pastoral methods.

We know that the sacraments produce supernatural life. But external reception is not necessary for "*in voto*" sacraments. We know, however, that good works to help our neighbor, both spiritually and materially, are definitely indispensable for supernatural life.

Apostolic action can be limited to reception of the sacraments. However, the practice of receiving the sacraments without performing good works is worth nothing. There can also be a concentration on good works, but without grace these works are not meritorious either. A good pastoral method with the sacraments as its starting point should culminate in works of charity, and a good pastoral method which begins with works of charity should culminate in the sacraments.

The only difference, but most important, is that reception of the sacraments does not presuppose good works. It is necessary to prove that there are good works, even though they are wholly interior, if we are to presume that there is supernatural life. "We know that we have passed from death to life, because we love the brethren" (1 Jn. 3, 14).

On the other hand, good works, whether internal or external, in behalf of one's neighbor, must be presumed as something performed by supernatural love. In order to presume the existence of supernatural life, it is necessary to believe that everybody is acting in good faith, so long as the opposite is not apparent.

Both ways are legitimate. However, insistence on good works seems more effective than insistence on the sacraments. But neither can we judge abstractly that someone who apparently has only received the sacraments has not performed good works which may be unknown to us or unknowable (interior), thus manifesting love for his neighbor.

What we are trying to clarify is the priority and the emphasis which everyone engaged in apostolic action should give to good works. This priority becomes more clearly apparent when considered in the light of two historical circumstances of our time: the social problem and pluralism. These are circumstances, moreover, which should orient pastoral action.

THE SOCIAL PROBLEM

On many occasions the social problem of our time has been defined from the Christian standpoint by the popes and by various authors. Material poverty is an unquestionable element in these definitions. It is not an exclusive factor, but it is a basic consideration if we are to understand the problem and solve it. In the modern world it is impossible to be a Christian if we do not fully understand the problem of material poverty. For, to solve this problem the assistance of all men is needed. Consequently, it is only in cases of special vocation or exceptional personal circumstances that we can exempt Christians from external and material good works in the modern situation. As a general policy, the apostolate should give priority to material works to help our fellow men, and thus be centered in a perspective of active charity here and now.

PLURALISM

Pluralism has also been recognized as a characteristic of modern society. This pluralism is both ideological and institutional. The religious, philosophical, and political systems which are opposed to pluralism have had to face the reality of its coexistence. This is an easier and less costly solution than mutual elimination. Coexistence can only be established on the basis of points in common. Action programs offer an important number of common points. But action in behalf of men, and carried out by men, is never totally good nor totally evil. When it really occurs, passing from mere projects to accomplished realities, it becomes a challenge to the consciences of all those who are seeking the good of humanity. The challenge of action is quite demanding; either we accept a program of action which implies acceptance of whatever inevitable defects there may be, or we reject it, which means that we are discarding the advantages and gains which it undeniably must also offer.

However, this action is something concrete. The variables which condition it are controllable, for the most part, by objective observation. Facts do not lend themselves to debate. Furthermore, this action, as service to others, has risen among the values of the modern world to the highest place. Both Christians and non-Christians accord first priority to it. The differences are in the means, the modalities, and the ultimate ends. But the principle of love of neighbor is not debatable. It is an essential element of Christianity and constitutes an element held in common by all men. We might perhaps say that in non-Christians this principle is natural in origin rather than formally Christian. But to make this statement, we would have to prove the bad faith professed by non-Christians, even when they are performing benevolent good works for their neighbor. If the Christian apostle concentrates his energies primarily but not exclusively on inspiring everyone to perform works of love for all men, he is then insisting on a value that is universally accepted and which constitutes a sign of the existence of supernatural life.

In a pluralistic world, united action in assisting other men is a unity which we may presume to be fundamentally Christian. Pope John XXIII affirmed this criterion in the encyclical *Pacem in Terris*.

The forms, conditions, and circumstances of this unity will be considered later in our study. For the moment, we need only stress the importance of insisting on external works in helping our neighbor as necessary for the apostle who must act in a pluralistic society. Benevolent works for our neighbor, from the theological point of view, constitute one of the surest signs of the existence of supernatural life. And from the pastoral standpoint, these good works constitute the most important objective for the apostle who lives in a pluralistic society with social problems.

2. *Factors of Economic Programming in Underdeveloped Countries*

CONCEPTS

The concept of economic programming must be clearly explained in order to enter into any consideration regarding it. Every program presupposes foresight of the future. It assumes that there is a plan. That is why it is necessary to define what we mean by economic planning and in what sense programming can be synonymous with planning.

Economic programming can be based on foresight which in no way assures fulfillment. But it can also be part of economic planning. In our present study it will be considered in this sense, and consequently we shall try to go deeply into the concept of planning. Economic planning comprises all the means and ends that are chosen for development of the goods and services of a particular society.

Economic planning can vary from one community to another, from one country to another, and from one socio-economic region to another. It can also vary in accordance with systems and the kind of authority which does the planning and execution. The variables are different in a socialist country, in a capitalist country, or in a country that is developed or developing.

PLANNING IN SOCIALIST COUNTRIES

Planning in socialist countries was more the result of needs than a policy premeditated by Marxist experts.

The Soviet Union had to take into account from the very beginning of the socialist system the penury of raw materials. It was necessary to centralize their distribution. This centralization and distribution in turn required a centralization of information. The work of the Council of National Economy, created by Lenin on February 5, 1918, was at first limited to the application to industry of the statistical questionnaires already utilized for agriculture over a long period in other countries. The government "Opportunity Service" made projections and predictions at the national level, which gradually were changed into directives. The Gosplan, a commission for State planning, began in 1923 to prepare Five-Year Plans for the metallurgical industry and the transport services. It was not until fifteen years later that the methods and theory for national planning were definitely established. It should be noted, however, that at the beginning the planning was carried out in keeping with the private ownership of most of the means of production. Therefore, it was not very different from the planning now undertaken in capitalist countries. It was only when the State controlled the principal means of production that it could begin planning with truly compelling power.

There has been much discussion concerning the possible economic evolution of Russia if it had remained within the capitalist system that was developing in the rest of Europe. However, this kind of thinking is unrealistic. We must abide by the facts and analyze them as they occurred historically. The Soviet Union, largely because of its system of economic planning, with State control of the means of production, has now become at least the second greatest economic power in the world, although it began as an underdeveloped country in the year 1917.

To what can we primarily attribute this development? Without overly restricting ourselves to the Marxist theory of plus-value, it can be stated that the Soviet Union has utilized almost in its totality and in a progressive manner the profits of national production for common purposes and projects that were technically planned. This result has a close causal connection with Marxist theory.

However, it is fitting to ask to what extent any other ideology, as for example an ideology of the spiritual type, could have inspired similar economic effects, and to what degree materialist principles are involved in the authoritarian orientation of investments. At the end of this chapter this problem will be considered.

PLANNING IN THE CAPITALIST COUNTRIES

Before the last World War, capitalist planning at the national level could only be found in Germany. With the exception of partial plans, it is only since that period that we find national economic planning in almost every country. The late appearance of this kind of planning can be attributed to the following causes:

1. sufficient resources with regard to raw materials;
2. the absence of regional integration, as demonstrated for instance in the European Common Market;
3. the lack of generalized planning at the company and local levels;
4. the absence of statistical data sufficiently complete and accurate;
5. the absence of a sufficiently interventionist conception of the State.

Economic planning in the capitalist countries, as also in the socialist countries, is an effect of economic development and of competition. However, in the capitalist countries which we are now considering, the characteristics of planning are still very different from those prevalent in socialist countries. "Production in a liberal system would be more in terms of private interests than general needs to which they are adapted only with difficulty," according to Campion (cf. *Planification: Dictionnaire des Sciences Economiques* [Paris, 1958]). In spite of this, we should note the manner in which general needs have been progressively more taken into account in the capitalist countries. In order to continue with this analysis, we should give some consideration to the evolution of the political structure of these same countries.

Soon after democratic regimes were established, the minority pressure groups oriented the economic policy. Economic development brought with it a social development characterized by an elevation of the cultural and economic levels of the majority groups. Marxist doctrine and the Social-Christian movement nourished the formation of popular organizations. The scarcity first of skilled labor, and later on of a national work force in general, made the national labor organizations more powerful.

With the rise in national income came an apparent elevation, although not proportionate, of the economic level of the majority groups. This facilitated the increase of the educational level and of cooperatives of every kind among these same groups which began to exercise various and effective pressures on governmental organisms. The play of forces between the minorities as holders of the economic power and the organized majorities became more equitable. Private interests became more general. Naturally, this occurred within national boundaries, because with regard to international policy the interests of the indigent countries were sacrificed to those of the rich countries. Lenin's prediction began to come true: national capitalism was changed into international imperialism.

The characteristic which fundamentally differentiates capitalist planning from socialist planning is the degree of control over investments and the rapidity with which such control is acquired. At the present time the control of investments in the capitalist countries, accomplished by indirect systems such as taxation, credit, subsidies, and so forth, is quite generalized. However, it never reaches the degree of intensity attained in the socialist countries. And private interests, although subject to intervention, are still very influential in political and policy decisions in general.

With regard to rapidity, it is certain that the acquisition of control in socialist countries required a process of several years. Nevertheless, the orientation towards common interests and the

112

technical standard were dominant from the start and the process was evidently of shorter duration.

PLANNING IN UNDERDEVELOPED COUNTRIES

Indigent countries have been called "underdeveloped countries," "developing countries," or "countries moving towards development." The various designations have finally acquired a euphemistic character more in accordance with paternalism than with any technical standard.

There are, of course, various degrees and stages of underdevelopment. However, an underdeveloped country is different from a *developing* country. The former is structurally unable to develop itself. The latter has already passed beyond the starting point of development. If the opposite were true, it could not be called a "developing country."

Planning in underdeveloped countries must now take advantage of the acquired experience of the capitalist countries and the socialist countries as well. In fact, the underdeveloped countries are now attempting the establishment of economic planning. In many of them, there are State planning organisms which are executing this economic planning with very little efficiency. Administrative formulas are proposed, experts assembled, and congresses held, all for the purpose of improving these efforts. However, it is essential that structural deficiencies be carefully studied because they create obstacles in these countries which prevent authentic and effective economic planning beneficial to the majority. Among these deficiencies there are two kinds of obstacles: the economic and the social. We shall take note of the principal obstacles:

1. lack of productive investments;
2. lack of technical personnel;
3. lack of development policy.

1. Lack of Productive Investments. Investments can be obtained from national capital or from foreign countries. The productive investments derived from national capital are difficult to obtain spontaneously. In the first place, national capital is scarce, since savings are small because incomes are low. Moreover, capital is invested by preference in countries that have a stable currency and in which there are greater institutional securities—that is, in industrialized and developed countries. These factors create vicious circles that are difficult to break.

Furthermore, investments in consumer and luxury goods are not planned nor are they always the most productive. Unfortunately, they are the most popular in the underdeveloped countries. In these countries it is impossible to make any productive investments if they depend on private initiative.

With regard to investment of foreign capital, the political factor is determinant. The division of the world into two camps, capitalist and socialist, means that the underdeveloped countries that are aligned with the one or the other are subjected to a monopoly insofar as external financing is concerned. The lack of competition which this polarization entails puts the underdeveloped countries unconditionally in a state of dependence on the investing country.

The planning of investments, whether national or foreign, now requires that they be done on the supranational level. All the underdeveloped countries hope to acquire their economic independence with the help of industrialization. Almost all of them also seek to possess heavy industry on a national scale. However, the isolated efforts of each nation can become uneconomical. Through regional integration, a study could be made of the kind of investments that would be most productive, and perhaps some of these countries could specialize in agricultural production and others could develop certain industries complementary to those of other countries. This supranational planning requires a margin of freedom so that the underdeveloped countries can profit from the play of competition established among the developed countries.

2. Lack of Technical Personnel. Technical personnel cannot be obtained without investments in the sector of education. The low budgets of underdeveloped countries for this purpose are a manifestation of the lack of any standard of productivity with regard to investments. There is a preference for investing in war matériel, in the army, or in a rather inefficient bureaucracy, since these investments are more in agreement with the interests of the privileged minorities who make such decisions.

With such low percentages of technical training, it is impossible to find competent executors for a really scientific development plan. The high amount of illiteracy is also a powerful influence. This fundamental defect logically influences the middle and upper levels of education. For lack of authoritative planning, the professionals of the higher level are sometimes more numerous than those of the middle level, although necessities require the very opposite. And the best skilled professionals often emigrate to developed countries where they receive higher pay.

On many occasions the help given by rich countries to those that are underdeveloped is largely in the form of technical assistance. This is very necessary, but it would also be most important to determine how to avoid the emigration of an underdeveloped country's own experts.

3. Lack of Development Policy. The lack of productive investments and of technical personnel is subject to a series of vicious circles from which it is impossible to emerge without a decision on the part of those who control the factors of power. In the underdeveloped countries, the various factors of power are generally concentrated in very few hands. The means of production and the high cultural levels belong to a minority ruling class.

This same class exercises political power by itself or through a body of politicians. In some countries in which there is a greater division of labor, the ruling class does not even assume the bother of exercising public functions. They are content to use their power to direct the public functionaries. The army is not justified in such countries except to maintain internal order, that is, the dominant structure. When we hear talk of frequent revolutions or *coups d'état* in Latin America for instance, it is not a question of real revolution, because the structures are preserved intact. All that happens is that there is barely a simple change of personnel in public offices. When this change cannot be carried out by the ruling class through legal means, then illegal procedures are chosen instead. Through economic, cultural, political, and military power, the ruling class controls all other power. In countries where Church and State are united, the Church is an instrument of the ruling élite. Moreover, when the Church possesses great economic power and controls the educational system, the Church is then sharing the power of the ruling minority.

We shall now try to determine what factors influence the economic decisions of the ruling minorities in the underdeveloped countries, and whether it is possible for measures to be taken to break the vicious circles. As an example, we shall consider the decisions taken with regard to investments, since on these the two first obstacles are dependent, that is, the lack of productive investments and technical personnel.

Decisions to make investments that would be beneficial to majorities can only be adopted with difficulty by the minorities unless they also can benefit by these same decisions. No doubt altruistic attitudes can be found in some members of the minority group. But it is difficult for individual motivations to produce group attitudes as such. We shall examine one decision that could be made by the minority class which would be beneficial to everyone. This would be a general raising of the standard of living.

116

In principle, the increase of purchasing power augments demand, and this growing demand will result in the increase of production. If this mechanism is to function, certain conditions are necessary:

1. the existence of a national market economy;
2. free competition—the absence of monopolies, cartels, and tariff protectionism;
3. a mentality of enterprise among producers.

We should try to explain these conditions. An important sector of the members of the ruling class in the underdeveloped countries do not derive their incomes from a national market economy. Absentee landlords, many ranch owners, and those who invest abroad, are not affected by the immediate fluctuations of the demand for goods and services within the internal market.

The concentration of economic power in few hands is correlative to the monopolistic structure. In the underdeveloped countries, the monopolies, trusts, and cartels control production, especially industrial production. With regard to agricultural production within a market economy, the middlemen enjoy a monopoly of distribution.

The monopolistic producer does not necessarily depend on the volume of demand to maintain his level of earnings. He can establish prices over and above the marginal costs of production. The volume of production will only increase when the advantages of mass production or a large quantity of sales justify a lowering of prices.

The raising of the standard of living can only be achieved by tapping the earnings of capitalists. It is much simpler to insist on higher prices for fewer consumers than lower prices for more consumers. The latter formula implies more labor, more possibilities of labor conflicts, and a reduction of luxury goods. If the monopolies enjoy the protection of the State, the competition of foreign products is then excluded. As long as the price of foreign products remains higher, the effort made by the national producer will be centered entirely on quality. Advertising will be directed to the sector of the population which consumes foreign products, for any reason whatever. The demand which is of interest to monopolists proceeds from higher economic strata. Producers can create an increase in the general standard of living only within a market of free competition.

With regard to an enterprise mentality among producers, and in spite of the limitations in the conditions just mentioned, it is undeniable that in the underdeveloped countries there are some producers who, within a market economy are in free competition. However, in deciding to increase the demand for their products, the producers must have a real desire to enlarge their production. And this requires the possession of an enterprise mentality in the sense in which Schumpeter defines it: placing productivity, creativity, and audacity in the foreground. Nevertheless, the spreading of this attitude is closely dependent on general economic development. There are two factors between which reciprocal causality exists. In the underdeveloped countries a feudal mentality is the most widespread. Prestige is based more on possession, and especially the possession of ostensible goods, than on producing or possessing the goods of production. This means that only a small minority of the producers is interested in raising the standard of living of the popular classes. This minority is commonly called a "progressive" or "nationalistic middle class."

The example of the decision outlined with regard to the standard of living shows us how difficult it is to persuade the ruling class to make decisions beneficial to the majorities rather than exclusively concerning their own interests. In the underdeveloped countries, the power of this class is so great that any concession is considered a damaging loss. It would be very hard for the ruling minorities to make a spontaneous effort to break through the vicious circles. That is why a development policy does not exist in the underdeveloped countries and why there cannot be real economic planning.

On analyzing the absence of a development policy, we saw the difficulty that prevents the ruling class from adopting technical standards to ensure the welfare of the majorities rather than their own class interests. If initiative does not proceed from the ruling class, it can be supposed that it will come from the majorities, as was explained in speaking of the developed capitalist countries.

However, it is difficult for the majorities in underdeveloped countries to exert sufficiently effective pressures to orient the policy of economic development. It is obvious that just as there is a difference in the degrees and stages of development, there will also be a difference in the possibilities of majority pressure to produce economic effects.

We should now consider the obstacles that must be overcome if the majorities are to exert pressure for exclusively economic effects. These obstacles generally are apparent in underdeveloped countries, but in different degrees. Among the principal obstacles, the following can be mentioned:

1. lack of motivation;
2. lack of information;
3. lack of organization;
4. lack of freedom of action.

1. Lack of Motivation. Motivation is directly related to antici-pated efficacy. Now, anticipated efficacy is dependent on experi-ence and information. Efficacious experience in economic matters is the result of other obstacles that will be considered later on, and the necessary information pertains to efficacy in other similar societies.

In general, the popular masses in the underdeveloped coun-tries have very little confidence in their own ability to accomplish structural economic reforms. However, they do have some con-

119

fidence, and therefore motivation, with regard to casual or superficial reforms.

2. Lack of Information. "Information" is taken here in the broadest sense as the possibility to read, hear, learn, and so forth.

The media of information of the popular majority classes are quite precarious. Because of the high rate of illiteracy, the auditory media have become most common, especially since the invention of transistors that do not require infrastructural functioning to produce energy. Personal contacts are also effective, although in these countries they are greatly hindered by the lack of transportation facilities.

The best media are those most suitable for transmitting or tuning in slogans that are more political than scientific. Information concerning economic matters does not occupy an important place in the news received by the popular masses in underdeveloped countries. Among the news broadcasts most of the references to economic matters pertain to the failures and troubles of labor unions which, in these countries, are quite frequent.

3. Lack of Organization. Organization presupposes planning and discipline, and these factors are really a by-product of development.

The underdeveloped countries have generally been dominated by developed countries. Various forms of colonialism have favored passivity in most of the colonial areas. Individualism, especially among the small landholding population of the countryside, was introduced at the same time as the colonial institutions.

Substructural organizations are scarce in the underdeveloped countries. The native "reservations" with their communal organization are gradually disappearing, especially in countries in which the ruling classes are more compact.

120

4. *Lack of Freedom of Action.* The activity of rural groups has always been difficult because of the dispersion and individualism which in general characterize their constituents. The most powerful groups from the numerical, economic, and organizational standpoint belong to the great enterprises, both urban and rural. Furthermore, the lower members of these enterprises generally share in the privileges of the owners and managers, although on a very inferior scale. In general, the labor unions of the great monopolistic or protected enterprises are company unions which enjoy no freedom of action.

The low economic resources of this basic population have impeded their freedom of action. The strikes of the non-company unions, when they are not declared illegal, are simply weakened through hunger.

Legal or informal persecution is an instrument of the ruling classes to hinder the activity of popular organizations and especially the activity of their leaders.

In conclusion, we may say that in the underdeveloped countries it will not be possible to form majority groups to produce any exclusively economic changes of a structural character without the elements and factors that are implicit in the process of development itself. Such factors primarily include an effective motivation to form the groups, certain and complete information, a sense of planning and discipline, and a relative political, legal, and economic freedom to undertake necessary changes.

THE POSSIBILITY OF POLITICAL PRESSURE FROM THE MAJORITIES IN UNDERDEVELOPED COUNTRIES

For pressures of a political type exerted by majorities, the obstacles in underdeveloped countries are much fewer. Political propaganda is more abundant and accessible, producing motivations based upon known results. Political organizations, on the contrary, fare with greater difficulty, but sometimes they can disguise themselves as social organizations and, in this case, clandestineness favors motivation. Freedom of action is also diminished and perhaps even more so than in the attempts to exert economic pressures. However, the struggle, precisely in order to win, although more obvious, changes into something less difficult.

Political pressure, of course, cannot be isolated from economic pressure, or even less from social pressure. However, political pressure is considered here in the sense of a series of actions, legal or illegal, peaceful or violent, which are undertaken to procure governmental decisions. These governmental decisions can pertain to structures, reforming or changing them. Consequently, pressure can be exerted either to obtain casual or superficial changes or to reform and even change the structures. This distinction is fundamental for underdeveloped countries.

Pressure to bring about superficial changes that are not structural has generally been the only activity of the organized majority groups. The establishment of labor legislation copied on that of the developed countries has served as a sophism of distraction to channel the efforts of the popular class towards superficialities. Among these casual or superficial changes there are a few economic advantages that should be included as results of the economic pressures already mentioned.

Pressure to obtain reformist changes has tried to provide solutions of transaction, that is, solutions which cover interests common to both the upper and the popular classes. These solutions do not change the structures, but merely adapt them to these common interests, if they exist at all. Sometimes they prepare the society for fundamental change, as for example the laws of agrarian reform which serve to industrialize a country.

Pressure to obtain a revolutionary change aims at a transformation of the structures themselves. In particular, this involves a change in the structure of property, income, investments, consumption, education, and in political and administrative organization. It also seeks change in international relations of a political, economic, and cultural kind.

The desire and foresight of the ruling class are modified by the type and intensity of pressure coming from the popular class. In the chart which follows on page 124 are listed the alternatives which this confrontation of attitudes and forces may offer.

EXPLANATION OF THE CHART

1. Values. Three levels of intensity are arbitrarily mentioned in terms of maximum, medium, and minimum.

2. Desire. This is not only a matter of traditional and sentimental attitude, nor of an attitude of isolated persons. The desire can be motivated for economic reasons and by group interests. In this outlook, the fear generated by the danger of not surviving as a class or as a group is excluded from the desire. This fear is mentioned in the section entitled "Foresight."

The desire was previously analyzed when we considered the common interests that can lead the ruling class to make decisions with regard to productive investments. Although there is a risk of generalizing arbitrarily, it can be stated that the degree of desire of the ruling class depends upon the number, the economic independence, the nationalism, and the enterprising mentality of its members. A progressive middle class can even desire a change of structures. However, this progressivism of the middle class is also a by-product of general development.

3. Foresight. This is a wholly intellectual and rational position. An event can be foreseen even though it is not desired. The attitude concerning structural changes can vary fundamentally if it is foreseen. Many decisions can be taken by the ruling class in virtue of the famous principle of "sacrificing something in order not to lose everything."

The foresight of the ruling class depends on two factors: the

POSSIBLE FORMS OF STRUCTURAL CHANGE

Ruling Class		Popular Class		
DESIRE	FORESIGHT	PRESSURE	RESULT	EXAMPLE
b	a	a	Peaceful Revolution	Chile
c	c	a	Violent Revolution	Cuba
c	b	b	Reformism	Colombia
c	a	b	Rightist *Coup d'État*	Brazil
c	a	c	Repression	Venezuela
b	b	b	Status Quo	Uruguay
a	a	a	Ideal Peaceful Revolution	?

VALUES: a = Maximum, b = Medium, c = Minimum

124

capacity for analysis and information. The capacity for analysis pertains to the qualifications and intelligence of their leaders. Information depends on the channels of communication. If one of these two factors is deficient, the foresight will also be deficient. That is why differences can be noted between the foresight of the ruling class and the real pressure of the popular class.

Unfortunately, in the underdeveloped countries deficiencies are possible in both factors. The average professional qualifications of the leaders can be quite low, especially in colonized countries in which the colonizing powers have impeded the higher education of the native cadres. In any case, it is very probable that the low qualifications of the leaders are attributable to the low general educational level which is characteristic of the underdeveloped countries. And this situation is aggravated when the most qualified leave to find work in the developed countries.

With regard to information, the problem in the underdeveloped countries which were colonies at some time or other is the coexistence of two cultures. Maurice Duverger classifies these two cultures in terms of "modern population" and "archaic population" (*La Influencia de las Fuerzas Políticas en la Administración Pública en los Países en Proceso de Desarrollo* [Bogotá, 1963], p. 18). Generally, the ruling minority is identified with the "modern population" and the popular majority with the "archaic population." It is this cultural division which is the principal obstacle with regard to information. The means of communication are constantly becoming more available to the popular class. But this communication increases the expectations of this class in a way that is disproportionately greater than the economic and social progress achieved. The institutions of communication are controlled by the ruling class, as for instance the press, radio, television, and so forth. The popular class has very few means of communication. This circumstance can produce information that is relatively useful with regard to the attitudes of the ruling class, but it can also prevent this ruling class from knowing what is actually happening among the majority groups. On many occasions, because of cultural differences, it is possible to use the same vocabulary with completely different meanings. And then, of course, the terminology will divide far more than it unites. And this can mean that a powerful fundamental pressure exists which is not foreseen by the ruling class.

4. *Pressure.* We have already explained the different kinds of pressure which the popular class can exert. In this outline, no attempt is made to indicate which of the three is exercised. However, the degree of intensity (a, b, c) refers to the efficacy with which structural change, properly so called, is sought.

5. *Result.* This can be doubtful, but the results that are listed can be considered as quite probable.

6. *Examples.* These are taken from Latin American cases that are best known to the author. They may not be wholly exact, but they are enlightening.

DEDUCTIONS

Study of the chart indicates the following conclusions.

1. In the underdeveloped countries structural changes will not be produced without pressure from the popular class.

2. Peaceful revolution is directly determined by the foresight of the ruling class, although the desire on the part of this class is difficult to arouse.

3. Violent revolution is a quite probable alternative, because the ruling classes find difficulty in the matter of foresight.

With regard to economic planning, we can affirm that it is very difficult to obtain any such planning that is technically oriented to benefit the majorities if there is no structural reform which permits these majorities to exert pressure on political decisions.

If the planning is not done by the State, compelling the orientation of investments, it is impossible to bring about any efficiency favorable to the majorities. That is why the problem for Christianity is stated in terms of efficacious charity, that is, in terms of that which constitutes the first priority in the apostolate of the modern world and of the underdeveloped countries.

3. Christian Responsibility in Economic Planning

THE PROBLEM

It has been shown that the modern apostolate, especially in underdeveloped countries, must have as its principal objective the attainment of charity that is really efficacious among all men, without distinction of creeds, attitudes, or cultures.

Furthermore, it seems practically impossible for majorities in the underdeveloped countries to attain a really human socioeconomic level unless there is economic planning to change the structures. These structures will not change without pressure from the majorities, and this pressure will be peaceful or violent depending upon the attitude of the minority ruling class.

With reference to this process, Christians must adopt an attitude that will not betray the practice of charity. Their reaction must not be opportunistic or expedient with regard to the needs and demands of the world. However, a Christian must not withdraw from the world, but rather protect himself from evil (Jn. 17, 15). He must sanctify the world in truth (Jn. 17, 19). Like Christ, he must become incarnate in humanity, and in its history and culture. Accordingly, he must forever seek the application of his life of supernatural love in the economic and social structures in which he should always be active.

HISTORICAL POSSIBILITIES OF ECONOMIC PLANNING THAT WILL BE BENEFICIAL TO THE MAJORITIES

When mention is made of a temporal undertaking carried out by Christians, every kind of integralism should be discarded, because this pertains to the activity of Christians as persons, as citizens of the world, and not as members of an institution and religious society. For this reason, it is not necessary to determine whether this activity can be confirmed and carried out by a political party that calls itself "Christian," or by any organization in which Christians participate. Instead, we must try to define the possibilities, and the advantages and disadvantages, if Christians assume leadership of technical planning that will benefit majorities in indigent countries.

1. Possibilities. Regardless of the advances achieved in recent times, we must admit that Christians have been far behind in the field of social accomplishments. Moreover, it has been only in recent times that technical and scientific orientation has been a part of the Christian heritage. Whether because of their compromises or their scientific qualifications, especially in underdeveloped countries, Christians do not generally deserve or cannot properly assume leadership in economic planning or structural reform.

This situation could change in the event that other ideological currents were halted in their activity or in their technical progress, and if Christians continued in their advance. However, this does not seem very likely.

2. Advantages. If Christians assumed leadership in the matter of change and in planning, it is possible that the ultimate ends might be quite compatible with a more integral humanism, and that the chosen means would be less traumatic, especially in relation to certain spiritual values.

3. Disadvantages. In view of the historical circumstances in which Christians find themselves, it is possible that they will fail for lack of technology and because of their monolithic dogmatism. This monolithic aspect, in the sense of excluding pluralism in their activity, deprives them of the assistance of many leaders of great scientific qualification. This exclusion cannot be permitted in countries in which there is precisely a lack of technical experts.

PLANNING DIRECTED BY MARXISTS

By Marxists we mean specifically those who adhere to historical and dialectical materialism. Among these are the orthodox Communists, whom we will investigate separately. First we shall consider Marxists who do not obey the discipline of the official Communist Party.

1. Possibilities. In the modern world, Marxists began the movement advocating structural change. They have technical experts in economics and in the physical and biological sciences. But dogmatism in the social sciences has been partially harmful to the orthodox Marxists who are the most emphatically dogmatic. We say "partially," because orthodox socio-economic analyses are in harmony with the socio-economic structures of the indigent countries. As a matter of fact, if we compare Marxist analyses strictly pertaining to the socio-economic structures of these countries with capitalist analyses, we will find that the Marxist analyses are better adapted to reality and especially to the expectations of the indigent majorities.

With reference to economic planning, Marxists have held the first place, but it is important to recognize the difference between the purely economic, administrative, and technical mechanism of economic planning which authoritatively regulates investments, and the philosophy which inspired this regulation. In our time, this same regulation is inspired and practiced by virtue of other philosophies, for example in Israel. This proves that it is not necessarily connected with Marxist ideology.

2. Advantages. Among the advantages of Marxist planning we should note its orientation, which is specifically popular, and the value of its analyses of underdeveloped or developing societies. We should also keep in mind its tradition in the struggle for structural change and technical planning.

3. Disadvantages. The orthodox Marxists run the risk of being dogmatic in socio-economic matters which are most complex, variable, and contingent. Likewise, with regard to tactics, the party members follow prefabricated schemes which in many cases, as in Cuba, oblige them to diverge from the revolutionary struggles that are not in keeping with these schemes.

With regard to heterodox Marxists, they can run the risk of pursuing truncated and diminished ends because they are confined within materialistic conceptions. As for the means employed, it is probable that many of them restrain and curb certain human rights.

PLANNING DIRECTED BY UNCOMMITTED PERSONS

1. Possibilities. The revolutionary struggle cannot be carried out unless there is a complete and integrated *Weltanschauung.* That is why it is difficult in the contemporary Western world for this struggle to be undertaken apart from Christian and Marxist ideologies which, for all practical purposes, are the only ideologies that possess an integral *Weltanschauung.* And for this reason it is difficult for uncommitted persons who do not belong to one of these ideological camps to assume revolutionary leadership. However, these persons can contribute usefully insofar as they are really committed, and to the extent that they are technical experts.

2. *Advantages.* Uncommitted persons have the advantage of stripping dogmatism from political struggles whenever these persons have real influence and are working in good faith.

3. *Disadvantages.* The two ideological extremes can be disadvantageous for those who are not working by virtue of a total conception of the problem, thus becoming "useful idiots" in one or the other of these sectors and working without any mystique.

THE CHRISTIAN ATTITUDE TOWARDS EFFORTS TO BRING ABOUT STRUCTURAL CHANGES AND ECONOMIC PLANNING FAVORABLE TO THE MAJORITIES

After what has been said, it remains quite clear that in poor countries the Christian not only can but must commit himself to the process of structural change in order to successfully undertake technical planning that is favorable to the majorities. In fact, for a Christian the greatest hesitation to adopt such an attitude would probably arise if the active pursuit of these objectives were directed by Marxists. In such a case, the Christian would have three alternatives: rejection of this action, abstention, and collaboration.

The choice to reject or abstain from activity which in itself would be beneficial to the majority should be seriously reflected upon by every Christian. To make such a decision, it would be necessary to show that the means employed are intrinsically evil or that there are inevitable ends which are also evil.

With regard to economic planning, the end principally sought is the control of earnings and investments. The means would be the intervention of the State insofar as this was necessary in the means of production. It is possible that this intervention would move towards nationalization of some or all of the means of production.

This end and these means are not inherently evil. Furthermore, if using these means and seeking this end is the best way to ensure the common good in a particular society in a particular historical era, collaboration in this effort becomes morally obligatory.

Finally, there is the problem of the other ends sought by Marxists and the other means which they use. Collaboration with Marxists implies a moral problem and a problem of tactics, which are closely connected. It is a moral problem if there are evil ends consequential to the essential end or if, in fact, evil means are utilized. If this is the case, rejection or abstention are still not necessary so long as nothing is known concerning the kind of evil that is avoided and what kind of causality the evil ends possess in relation to good ends—whether efficient, total, or essential causality. In the historical reality of the underdeveloped countries, these circumstances are difficult to observe or prove. Revolution is such a complex undertaking that it would be deceitful to classify it within a system of causality and finality that is wholly evil. The means can be diverse, and in the course of action it is easy to introduce modifications.

With regard to the problem of tactics, we must ask whether, in a process which in itself is just, Christians, in deliberate and technical collaboration, could not simply disregard evil means and ends. If the Marxist problematic is closely analyzed, I believe that an affirmative answer is possible. Dialectical and historical materialism in the mental process of Marxists appears to be so useful for revolutionary methods that it can be considered as quite objective. Moreover, the materialistic focus gives Marxists a tendency towards the positive.

If the application of economic and social principles turns out well, it is probable that the insistence on philosophical speculation will fade out. As a matter of fact, this has already happened in certain places, as for instance in Poland. What is more, the most recent statements of Togliatti concerning anti-religious tactics show how Marxism must evolve in its theory, if in practice it is shown that religion is not "the opium of the people."

To undertake the collaboration that has been suggested, certain norms must be taken into account so as not to run the risk of serving as "useful idiots." It is therefore important that collaboration be established at the level of action where the scope and the doctrinal implications can be limited. We must be well-informed about the most efficacious ends and means in accordance with the technique and the circumstances, and we must also know the ends and means which correspond to the Marxist theory.

With firm decision and without timidity, we should enter into this collaboration, since the greatest authority accepted by the society that needs structural change is the authority of revolutionary commitment which, for the Christian, should be a commitment in charity. This authority will permit us to demand concessions in the event that Marxists have some share of power.

4. Conclusions

To seek authoritative economic planning in the indigent countries is generally an obligation for the Christian. This planning is essential to efficacy in the authentic service of the majorities and therefore it is a condition of charity in these countries.

It is most probable that the Marxists will take over the leadership of this planning. In this case, the Christian must collaborate insofar as his moral principles will permit, keeping in mind the obligation of avoiding greater evils and of seeking the common good. Under such conditions, it is possible that in the underdeveloped countries there will be no recurrence of the struggles among groups seeking structural reforms favorable to the majorities. Without factionalism, and without conquerors or conquered, Christians will be able to participate in the building of a better world that will continually draw closer to its ideal of universal love.

XIII.
CRITICISM AND SELF-CRITICISM

We shall have to convince ourselves that mankind is not seeking conflict. In fact, it is trying to avoid it as far as possible. Conflict is the result of a very complex series of factors, among which the will to cause it is perhaps the least influential. Those who are interested in studying the causes of human behavior must regard conflict as an object of study more than a manifestation of morality or immorality.

Dr. Carlos Lleras is an intelligent person, educated, and to say the least, highly civilized. That is why he seeks to enter into dialogue even with his greatest adversaries. He knows that dialogue is constructive, and for that reason he came to the University. The students like to hear him talk and they also like to ask him questions; in a word, they like the dialogue. And dialogue is one of the principal activities of a student. We can say for certain that the university student does not like the smell of tear gas, or throwing eggs at his fellow men, or spending his spare time exposing his personal safety to the fury of bayonets. And yet conflict occurred, and this was a conflict which, in itself, neither of the two parties sought or wanted. To explain this fact, we must try to see what currents were clashing and what they represented in themselves.

Quite apart from what they are in reality, the concept which the one holds regarding the other is for each of these social groups a stereotype, that is, a simplified figure of those external traits which make the greatest impressions. Carlos Lleras may possess both subjective and objective qualities. Nevertheless, like any man in politics, he represents a system, and, like the most characteristic politicians of the system, he personifies a class

135

which, in this case, is the privileged and governing minority. Theoretically, university students should study, do research, attend class, and nothing more. In an underdeveloped country, students combine in themselves two qualities which are rarely found conjoined in other groups of society: a relatively high cultural level, and a certain freedom in relation to the dominant structures and the ruling minority. This explains the political role which the university has played in underdeveloped countries and especially in Latin America. We are not concerned about anathematizing or praising the political intervention of university students. We must simply accept this intervention as a fact and explain the causes.

The two characteristics previously noted produce an attitude of defiance and nonconformity in a society whose structures require a fundamental change. In the more advanced democracies, defiance and nonconformity have their own channels of expression. Information is not a monopoly, as in the underdeveloped countries, even when there is an apparent freedom of opinion, expression, and press in these countries. The minority pressure groups have found methods that are less obvious and more efficacious than censorship and direct persecution. The blockading of propaganda, of job opportunities, and of financial support, produce not only the limitation but even the disappearance of all manifestations of opposition. When the institutional channels of expression are obstructed and nonconformity cannot be expressed, even if its intensity is increasing, this need for expression will follow riverbeds that are not foreseen among the structures in force. These channels are critically called "antisocial" or "pathological." At the moment when the possibility of using anti-social channels of expression of nonconformity coincides with the presence of the latter's object, a conflict is produced which is necessarily qualified as anti-social by the group that controls the institutional channels. The attitude of this ruling group is of course explainable. Unfortunately, it implies an absolute lack of self-criticism.

The errors of the ruling class are not sufficient per se to

produce a conflict. But the lack of self-criticism holds in error whoever falls into it. Regrettably, this has been one of the characteristics of the dominant class in recent years. The phenomenon of violence arises and, before carefully examining it, repression is sought as the only method to cope with it. When, after thirteen years of enduring this situation, someone dares to make a study of violence and publish it as an article, it does not produce any kind of serious thought, but instead is utilized as the instrument of some partisan group, or else is considered as an insult to another group. When the majorities refuse to vote in certain elections, this phenomenon is attributed to everything except the errors of the ruling class, and when social facts are revealed that are interpreted detrimentally to this class, it reacts immediately with defense and attack. This same written article will produce neither reflection nor self-criticism. It will only be an object of condemnation on the part of the ruling class, which will remain enclosed in its ivory tower and whose members will go on mutually praising one another. No censor will consider himself sufficiently authorized to contradict them. The chasm between this class and the popular majorities is continually deepened and the systems of communication between the two become more precarious every day.

The reforms that could prevent violent revolution are not initiated by the dominant class if the latter does not foresee greater evils in the future. Now the capacity of foresight is directly related to analytical ability and to the accuracy of information concerning the probability of these greater evils. Our ruling class simply lacks the ability to make an objective analysis. Sentiment and tradition generally orient all their reactions. The information media function from top to bottom, from the ruling class to the popular class, but not inversely, for lack of any means of expression and because of the differences in terminology.

These circumstances lead to paradoxical situations. The ruling group cannot understand why the University students, who are the most select among Colombian students, will not accept a rational dialogue. The University students do not understand why they meet with approval when they shout and throw rocks at Rojas Pinilla while they are censured when they hurl eggs at Carlos Lleras. The ruling group simply cannot understand why the University students mix into politics, but the students cannot understand why apolitical directives of the University allow a political conference within its own confines. The students fail to understand why the University's extraterritoriality was defended when the servants of the dictatorship were killing students within the White City, and now leans on the army to repress those who were considered the "traditional defenders of democracy." The double standard which the ruling class wishes to impose on the country is based upon their ignorance of the capacity for criticism which the popular class and the University students acquired as soon as they were able to express it. Only a brave and sincere self-criticism by the ruling class will make it possible to establish contact between the two classes. Whether this contact is re-established or definitively disappears will determine whether the next social conflicts in Colombia will culminate in agreement or violence.

XIV.
LETTER TO BISHOP RUBEN ISAZA

Your Excellency:

In addressing you, I am using the traditional form, although this does not signify anything contrary to the fraternal spirit that inspired this letter to an older brother whom God, in his providence, has placed in my life to represent him.

When Your Excellency suggested that I withdraw from my present work in order to make an inquiry concerning necessary steps to take in planning a pastoral program in our archdiocese, I asked for a little time before acceding to this request. The arguments I offered were based on motives of charity for many persons who depended on my work and whose situation would be most uncertain in the event that I withdrew immediately. I believe that these arguments were valid and Your Excellency agreed.

Without in any way diminishing their validity, I have since given much thought to the deep personal reaction which your proposal produced in me. The idea of working with the clerical structure of our Church was most repugnant to me.

I used the time of my spiritual retreat to consider this reaction more deeply. In a priest it may seem, if not absurd, at least improper.

My work as a priest has continued for more than ten years under the authority of my bishop, but somewhat apart from the clerical structure. This situation has doubtless created obstacles to my priestly spirit but it may also have produced certain advantages for the life of the Church. One of these advantages could be my acquisition of a more objective vision of the structure to which I belong but in which I have participated less than others. Perhaps these others, because of their abilities, may have a greater capacity for analysis, although they are more involved in the phenomenon that I am trying to describe.

When I thought about the possibility of working in the Curia, making an inquiry for them, I felt sure that I would be separating myself from the world and from the poor, thus including myself in a closed group whose organization belongs to the powerful of this world.

When I realized how I would have to direct the inquiry, certain theoretical problems arose. The solutions, I believe, would be expressed in a different sense or even be opposed to that of the hierarchy who would have to utilize the data which I investigated.

The solution of these problems which is vital for the success of the inquiry, since its orientation depends on it, and because it is impossible to investigate everything, means that the results must necessarily correspond to a common problematic between the investigator and those who have the responsibility for planning a pastoral program in the archdiocese.

With regard to my personal problematic, I want to write to Your Excellency in the hope that you will decide whether I am the right person to make the suggested inquiry.

In referring to a pastoral program, I mean all of the activities that are needed to introduce or extend the kingdom of God in a particular society and in a particular historical era. In order to reach an agreement concerning the essence of the pastoral program, we must agree on what the kingdom of God really is. And to orient an inquiry there must be agreement on a whole series of hypotheses concerning Colombian society in our time.

The kingdom of God is supernatural life and the justification of mankind. To extend the kingdom of God or establish it is a problem of life. Those activities which must be performed to introduce the kingdom are those which lead more surely and more effectively to life itself.

Among those activities there are a few priorities. In my

opinion, the emphasis which must be placed on means to establish the kingdom should be pursued in the following order, noting that these means do not exclude one another but are complementary.

—We must lead the people to love, and this must be a self-giving love (agape).
—Preaching the Gospel.
—External worship. The Eucharist and the sacraments (sacramentals—extraliturgical devotions).

Colombian society is largely a Catholic society insofar as it complies with external worship (baptism, confession, Communion, matrimony, burial, Mass, extreme unction, processions, novenas, scapulars, first Fridays).

Colombian society for the most part is ignorant of Catholic doctrine, although our people know a few catechism responses by memory.

Among the Colombian people there are many who love their fellow men with self-giving love, and yet they deny that they are Catholics, or in any case they repudiate adherence to the Church. When they speak of the Church, they mean its clerical structure.

If the pastoral effort merely concentrates on preserving the previous situation, it is possible that it will not achieve the establishment or extension of the kingdom of God.

If the priority of love is accepted above all else, and if preaching takes precedence over the activity of worship, then the hierarchy can be induced to authorize a pastoral mission.

Pastoral mission requires an emphasis on quality rather than quantity. There should be greater insistence on personal convictions than on family and social pressures. An exclusive Church-related educational system must be abandoned and pluralism should be accepted. Professional and curricular freedom should be allowed. Biblical catechetics can be provided for both children and adults. Self-giving must be stressed more than

141

faith and practice. And preaching of the Gospel must be emphasized more than external worship. There ought to be an elimination of the social and psychological factors which hinder a conscious and personal adherence to the Church among those who desire to love and serve their fellow men. Among these factors are the economic power of the Church and its political power. This is manifested formally through laws and the Concordat, and informally by clericalism (meddling in temporal matters with a domineering spirit). Among other factors we should mention the cultural, sociological, and psychological separation between the clergy and the faithful, the lack of solidarity with the poor, and the lack of scientific spirit in the Church.

If the pastoral mission that is proposed is a pastoral effort of conservation, it would be very difficult for me to collaborate in an effective way. I would do so through obedience, but counter to my rational convictions. As a matter of basic honesty, I want to bring these points to the attention of Your Excellency.

I am attaching an essay which I wrote on the primacy of charity.

I believe that my previous positions can either be supported theologically or else they constitute working hypotheses that can be verified by empirical inquiries. However, I am willing to retract my positions whenever I am convicted of error, and to make my submission if it is a matter of something contrary to dogma or to good custom.

I am Your Excellency's devoted servant,

Fraternally

XV.
PLATFORM OF THE UNITED FRONT
OF THE COLOMBIAN PEOPLE

To all Colombians, the popular classes, the organizations of communal action, labor unions, cooperatives, mutual aid societies, peasant leagues, Indian communities, and worker organizations, and to all nonconformists and those who are not aligned with the traditional political parties, we present the following platform to unify all sectors of the Colombian populace with concrete objectives.

1. Motives

1. The decisions that are indispensable for our Colombian political system, if it is to be oriented for the benefit of the majorities rather than the minorities, must be made by those who hold power.

2. Those who now possess real power constitute an economic minority who make all the fundamental decisions concerning national policy.

3. This minority never makes any decisions which might adversely affect their own interests or the foreign interests with which they are connected.

4. The decisions required for a socio-economic development of the country beneficial to the majorities and for national independence necessarily affect the interest of the economic minority.

5. These circumstances make a structural change of political power absolutely indispensable in order that the majorities may make the decisions.

6. At the present time the majorities reject the political parties and reject the system in force, but they do not have a political apparatus that is capable of seizing power.

7. The political apparatus that is organized must seek the greatest possible support from the masses. It will need technical planning and should be based upon principles of action rather than upon a popular leader so that the danger of "kitchen cabinets," demagogy, and personalism may be avoided.

2. Objectives

1. AGRARIAN REFORM

Ownership of the land will be vested in those who are working it directly.

The government will appoint agrarian inspectors who will deliver titles to the peasants but will require that cultivation be controlled by cooperative and communal systems in accordance with a national agrarian plan, and with credit and technical assistance.

Land will not be purchased by anyone. Any land that is necessary for the common good will be expropriated without compensation.

The Indian councils will enter into real possession of the lands which belong to them. This will promote the development and strengthening of these native communities.

2. URBAN REFORM

All those who are living in houses in cities and towns will be owners of the house which they inhabit. Persons who depend only on the rental of a house as a source of income may keep it, even if they are not living in it, if they can prove that such dependence is the case.

An owner will be fined if, in the judgment of the government, his house is not sufficiently utilized. This fine will be invested by the State in its housing projects.

3. PLANNING

An obligatory plan will be prepared with the aim of reducing imports, increasing exports, and industrializing the country.

All public or private investment will be subject to the national investment policy. Operations in foreign currencies will be handled exclusively by the State.

4. TAXATION POLICY

A progressive income tax will be collected from those whose earnings are greater than the income required by an average Colombian family to live decently, as for instance five thousand pesos in 1965. Anything more than this limit which is not invested in sectors indicated by the official investment policy will be completely surrendered to the State. No institution will be exempt from taxation. Wages up to a certain limit, for example five thousand pesos a month in 1965, will not be taxed.

5. NATIONALIZATION

Banks, insurance companies, hospitals, clinics, centers for the manufacture and distribution of drugs, public transportation facilities, radio and television, and natural resources will belong to the State.

The State will provide free education for all Colombians, respecting the ideology of the fathers of families until the end of secondary education, and the ideology of students after the secondary level.

Education will be obligatory until secondary or technical education is completed. There will be penal sanctions against fathers who do not comply with the obligation of educating their children. Financing will be covered by the official investment policy through increase of taxation.

Underground resources will belong to the State and the exploitation of oil will be undertaken in the interests of the national economy. Oil concessions will not be given to foreign firms except under the following conditions:

1. The participation of the State will not be less than 70%.
2. Refining, distribution, and production of fuels will be public services under State control.
3. After a period of not more than 25 years, there will be reversion to the State of all enterprises, equipment, and installations, without compensation.
4. Wages and salaries of Colombian workers and employees will be at least equal to those of foreigners of the same occupational categories.

6. INTERNATIONAL RELATIONS

Colombia will enter into relations with all the countries of the world and will foster commercial and cultural exchanges on conditions of equity and mutual benefit.

7. SOCIAL SECURITY AND PUBLIC HEALTH

The State will introduce a complete and progressive program of social security which guarantees the population the right to free health and medical attention, without prejudice to the private practice of the profession, and will carefully examine all the aspects related to unemployment, invalidism, old age, and death. All personnel of the health professions will be employed by the government and will be paid up to the limit fixed by law in accordance with the number of families who ask to be under their care.

8. FAMILY POLICY

There will be sanctions against fathers of abandoned children. The protection of the wife and children will be assured by law through effective sanctions.

9. ARMED FORCES

The budget for the armed forces shall be adequate for their purpose without affecting the health and educational needs of all Colombians. The defense of national sovereignty will be the responsibility of the whole Colombian nation. Women will be obliged to render some public service after they are eighteen years old.

10. WOMEN'S RIGHTS

Women will participate on an equal footing with men in the economic, political, and social activities of the country.

This platform was discussed, approved, and expanded by the popular sectors interested in it after it was publicly presented by Father Camilo Torres on May 22nd, 1965, a day on which the National United Front honored him at University City in Bogotá. Father Camilo Torres declared that, as a Colombian, as a sociologist, as a Christian, and as a priest, he was a revolutionary.

As a Colombian, because he could not disregard the struggles of his people.

As a sociologist, because through his scientific knowledge of reality he had reached the conviction that technical and effective solutions could not be achieved without a revolution.

As a Christian, because the essence of Christianity is the love of neighbor, and only by revolution could the good of the majority be achieved.

As a priest, because devotion to one's neighbor, which the revolution requires, was a requisite of fraternal charity and indispensable for complete fulfillment of his mission.

XVI.
COMMUNISM IN THE CHURCH?

What is your opinion concerning the revelation made by President Valencia concerning Communist infiltration in the Church?

From a strictly theoretical point of view, when we speak of the Church we speak of everyone who is baptized either by sacrament or by desire. This includes a large part of humanity, supposing that everyone of good faith has had a baptism of desire. In this sense I do not think that one can speak of Communist infiltration into the Church, since I think that in Colombia a large percentage of the Communists are baptized.

If we speak of infiltration, it is more logical to suppose that there are members of the Church who, calling themselves Catholics, are really Communists. To verify this, all that would have to be done would be to establish a tribunal, such as the old tribunal of the Inquisition, to weed out the Communist infiltrators within the Church.

However, in ordinary vernacular when one speaks of the Colombian Church, one means the bishops and priests, and thus the popular meaning, when speaking of infiltrators within the Church, is infiltrators within the clergy. To undertake an investigation that could possibly clarify this situation presupposes that it might at the same time establish the attitude within the Church that to have an opinion of one's own is a crime. It could be that the President did not have this intention in making his speech, but if it were taken seriously, the effects could not be any different.

According to your criteria, what is the cause for the frequent articles of a certain newspaper on the presence of Communist priests?

To be able to understand the motives behind a certain newspaper's writings about Communist priests, we shall have to analyze the "watchdog" phenomenon in general. Any ruling class has defense systems, some informal and others formal. In the case of an unpopular and minority ruling class, it is necessary to seek effective means to disqualify their adversaries in public opinion. Public opinion is more easily oriented with adjectives than with philosophical discussions.

To discredit a source it is enough to affix the epithet of "rotten." To have a dog chased away, although it may be in fine condition, it is enough to give it the adjective "rabid." In the early part of our era, to address an individual as "Christian" was a means of placing him outside of the law. Later, the enemy of the Roman Empire was called "barbarian" to justify his persecution. Before the French Revolution, free-thinkers, liberals, democrats, plebians, and so forth, were persecuted. Today, the best way to unleash persecution against an element dangerous to the ruling class is to call it "Communist."

The Colombian ruling class has considered the Church and the army its unconditional allies, and it is natural that when nonconformist priests or military men appear, this class feels that its internal structure is beginning to fall apart. Therefore, the nonconformist priests or military men constitute a much more dangerous element to the system than do Communists affiliated to the party. From this follows the necessity for the ruling class to discredit them, branding them as Communists. The press, servant to this class, cannot adopt a different policy.

Is the Colombian clergy guilty of Communism or anti-Communism?

The Colombian clergy is certainly not guilty of Communism. Communism holds a philosophical system incompatible with Christianity, although in its socio-economic aspirations most of its postulates do not conflict with Christian faith.

To say that it is guilty of anti-Communism, it would be necessary to study the pastoral letters, the writings, and the sermons of our bishops and priests. However, I personally feel that Communism has been considered as the main evil of Christianity in our time. This is a very untheological and unscientific approach.

Untheological because the main evil of Christianity is the lack of love, within the Church itself as well as with respect to the non-Christians, including Communists. Communism as a solution, with all its wisdom and all its errors, has arisen from the lack of an efficacious love applied in temporal structures in a scientific form by the Christians.

From the scientific point of view, the Christian should not be against, but rather, for the well-being of humanity. If this well-being cannot be brought about without changing the temporal structures, it would be sinful for the Christian to oppose the change. Only the discriminate and scientific criticism of Communism, with a view to the well-being of humanity, could justify, not an anti-Communistic, but a scientific stand, implying a rejection of everything that may be non-scientific.

According to your judgment, does the attitude of the Colombian clergy faced with social problems require a change?

In general I think that the attitude of the Colombian clergy faced with social problems does require a change. This change could be summed up in the following way:

1. Greater concern for the well-being of humanity rather than for preserving it from Communism.

2. Discard occasional and paternalistic charity as an habitual form of action.

3. Concentrate forces on the formation of a secular body capable of fundamentally transforming temporal structures, attacking in this way the origin of the social problems.

Does the Colombian clergy have a capitalist mentality?

To be able to judge the mentality of a social group, a fairly profound analysis is necessary. However, I feel that the Colombian clergy, at least in the impression it gives the public, appears to be more feudal than capitalistic and, in the best of cases, to have a clearly capitalist mentality.

Basically, the feudal mentality is characterized by the desire for possession, ignoring profit, productivity, and service to the community. The capitalist mentality is characterized by the desire for profit without considering service to the community. To the public the Colombian clergy appears as a group with the desire for possession. In the more important hierarchical circles and mainly in the urban centers, I think that it appears as a group with a desire for profit. The Colombian public, it seems to me, is not conscious of the fact that the Church spends money in the service of the community.

Should Communism be outlawed?

From a theoretical point of view, I think the best weapons to fight ideas are ideas. The best weapon in fighting political movements is to demonstrate greater effectiveness in the use of power. Therefore, legal orders opposing certain ideas or political movements are, in my opinion, a show of weakness against them.

However, if the Communists in a country are considered to

be excluded from public office, from the right to be elected, if they are excluded from university posts and in many cases lose the right to study and to work, it would be a less hypocritical position to officially declare them outlaws than to maintain an apparent legality, which is just a tactic to disguise this state of affairs in democratic robes in order to avoid having the adversaries capitalize on the mystique which illegality and victimization would lend them.

XVII.
POSSIBILITIES FOR THE LEFT

What are the predominant political criteria in Latin America?

Underdeveloped countries are characterized by the lack of industry, which presupposes division of labor, specialization, and rationalization of human activity. Relations which sociologists call "primary," that is to say, face-to-face relations of greater intimacy and depth, such as family and friend relationships, constitute the main factor in social life in underdeveloped countries. Sentiment and tradition govern almost all the institutions, including the political. To associate through programs with the different political trends is much less common than to support the leaders. Change of political affiliation from one generation to the next or within the period of a person's life is considered treason.

In countries that are classified as underdeveloped but in which political formation is more advanced, we encounter a greater influence of ideology and rational elements. However, this influence is exercised on a normal plane of speculative theories. The underdeveloped countries that were colonized by the West, by such deep-rooted philosophical and Cartesian cultures as the Spanish, have difficulty in adopting empirical and positive values.

Latin American countries in general, and especially those who have had at the same time a new and reduced immigration and a relatively large indigenous or mixed population, face the problem of the coexistence of two cultures within the same nation. One culture, typically Western, is based on a system of patrimony of a small privileged class descendent from the creole; the other culture is of mixed type, composed of both indigenous elements and Western elements in proportions which vary from country to country.

The process of acculturation of the indigenous or mixed masses has followed general laws. Material acculturation has been imposed, while non-material acculturation has taken place largely in exterior form only. We Latin Americans have received judicial, political, religious, and economic institutions in their exterior form—at least in reference to the lower class—without having assimilated the content of these institutions into our values and modes of conduct.

When the creoles, who had their own culture along with Western bourgeois capitalist problems, had to face the emancipation movement, they could not respond suitably to the reality of the masses but rather offered only imported solutions. Thus a movement of such popular origin as that of the Commoners in Colombia received no help from the creole bourgeois, who were occupied in the translation and spreading of the Western-originated "rights of man," and who later lost precious moments towards our Independence debating concepts copied from abroad such as federalism and centralism. The "Patria Boba," which embodied the traditional ideological colonialism of our ruling class, has been prolonged in less obvious forms to this day.

The predominant political criteria in underdeveloped countries, then, are: the sentimental and traditional, the normative and speculative, and those emanating from an ideological colonialism.

How do you see our political parties?

The political parties in Colombia have been a reflection of the criteria just mentioned. They copied in principle the denominational patterns and philosophies of the parties already created in Europe. However, in principle some socio-economic fundamentals were found to establish the difference between Liberals and Conservatives. Today, religious and ideological differences as well as socio-economic differences have practically disappeared.

From 1930 on, partisan competition began to concentrate around the bureaucratic and budgetary pork barrel, competition which grew with the multiplication of the budgetary figure following the tax reforms of 1936. The survival of the two traditional parties in Colombia must be explained by functional factors useful to the ruling class as well as to the popular class.

In every society, belonging to a group provides personal security. This phenomenon is even more noticeable in the societies of underdeveloped countries where formal institutions for personal and social security are lacking. In Colombia, to belong to one of the traditional parties is a form of acquiring security. If, moreover, the party is one of the few multi-class groups, in which the private citizen finds elements of identification with members of the highest social class, the function of providing security is often more important. Add to this the sentimental and traditional element, with the psychological and sociological security it brings, and we understand the importance which the political parties have for the popular class.

The ruling classes constituted a minority representing conflicting philosophical and socio-economic interests, interests which were grasped by the masses only in their most rudimentary and irrational forms. When these conflicts between the ruling classes disappeared, political affiliation constituted a traditional type link with the popular class. When social and economic problems worsened in the entire world and in Colombia, the Liberal-Conservative problem began to transform itself into a class problem.

By dividing Colombian society vertically and by grouping the popular class in the electoral struggles into opposing factions of sentiment and tradition, the political parties impeded the formation of a class party. The absence of such a party insured the privileges of the ruling class and its domination over the majority and popular classes. Thus while the political party in Colombia gives a psychological security to the popular class, it also gives socio-economic security to the ruling class.

In addition to this, we must add that in any multi-class group the indispensable condition for social ascent is conformity. The

156

demand for conformity is the most efficient instrument of control by a privileged minority on the majority, and as one ascends in the political hierarchy greater conformity is demanded.

The National Front is the result of the rationalization of a conflict, a conflict of sentiment, and a conflict concerning control of the budget and distribution of the bureaucratic pork barrel. The consequences of this conflict, violence and ineffective administration by military government, forced the leaders of both traditional parties to put aside their feelings and to come to agreement on what constituted the apple of discord: budget and bureaucracy. Reciprocal succession and parity of the parties in government were a double effect instrument, for they executed the distribution contract and guaranteed the continuing division of the popular class by sentiment and tradition. The objectives succeeded very quickly. However, the National Front, which as the first class party in Colombia constitutes a significant landmark in our political history, began to conciliate as a reaction the formation of another class party, that of the popular class.

What do you think of our progressive movements?

Political criteria predominant in underdeveloped countries have conditioned the orientation of those who have been called Leftist Colombian groups. In many cases our progressive leaders bind themselves to an altruist sentiment lacking scientific basis or rationally established tactics which we can identify with that of utopian socialists.

Traditionalism works in them not by action but by reaction. Though the traditional may appear advisable scientifically, it is often rejected through resentment. The normative and speculative spirit makes these same leaders lay emphasis on theoretical planning rather than on developing practical solutions to our socio-economic problems. This orientation is closely linked to the ideological colonialism of our Left. Slogans and clichés are used. A special revolutionary jargon is employed. Superficial solutions to Colombian problems are given. Public demonstrations of solidarity with the oppressed of foreign countries are made, while the situation of the national oppressed is forgotten. Sentimentalism also is translated into personal leadership and frustration. While the minority but all-powerful ruling class unites to defend its interests, Leftist leaders attack each other, causing confusion in the popular class, and represent in more faithful form the traditional, sentimental, and speculative criteria and that of ideological colonialism.

Are there any possibilities of full integration?

The Colombian popular class has been able to detach themselves from the political criteria predominant in the underdeveloped countries much faster than the Leftist leaders. Some historical circumstances of our national life have brought about the maturation of the political attitudes and conceptions of this class. Violence determined a grass-roots break with social isolation, a conflict between the country-dweller and the ruling class, a break with our sentimental and traditional values, a more positive and empirical conception of their [the popular class'] problems and, along the same lines, of the national problems; and from all this a beginning of the formation of class-consciousness.

The National Front polarized the discontent, now not towards an individual, a government, or a party, but rather towards a system, a ruling class. The official and private communal action programs, the technical assistance brought by agrarian reform, and other official and private programs helped to awaken, along with the consciousness of their own needs, a class consciousness. They have created security in the popular groups, they have begun to form habits of organization and self-leadership in the labor and farming communities.

The popular class seems disillusioned with the democratic electoral systems and so it boycotts the electoral assemblies. It does not consider itself represented by the leaders of the Left whose problematic seems unsuitable and whose interests are often egotistical. The popular class more and more trusts in itself and distrusts the elements of the other classes.

It is necessary for the intellectuals who desire the well-being of the popular class to be aware of their responsibility in the political and social opportunity of the moment. The people need concrete, national objectives of socio-economic development. The people need unity around technical and rational bases. The people need a group of leaders whose problematic is essentially realistic and adapted to the concrete Colombian circumstances. Leaders who are capable of abandoning all personalism for the attainment of a scientific ideal. Leaders who are capable of abandoning all traditional and sentimental elements not justified by technology. Leaders capable of abstracting from philosophical and normative elements, not in their personal life nor in their ultimate objectives, but with regard to their representation of the disjointed elements among all those who seek concrete and scientifically justified action in favor of the majorities and in favor of the country. Leaders who are capable of abstracting from imported theoretical schemes, and of utilizing their capabilities to seek Colombian paths for a definitive and solid transformation of our institutions.

XVIII.
EXPROPRIATING CHURCH PROPERTY

In your thesis, do you not think that the application of agrarian reform is revolutionary?

I don't think the application is revolutionary because the law is not revolutionary. I think that the law is a compromise between our ruling classes within which we find that the progressive industrialists have drawn up a law which is more for agrarian fomentation than for agrarian reform, because land is paid for at commercial prices. Land can be reserved up to 100 hectares, which in many cases is excessive—in the cases, for example, of the irrigation districts. Besides this, there is no obligation to reinvest the high prices paid for the land back into the country. Besides the irrigation districts, we also have property that could quite adequately be exploited but cannot be expropriated. So, with all these limitations, the Colombian Institute for Agrarian Reform (INCORA) has to confine itself to the irrigation districts to increase the national income and modernize agriculture. But it cannot really bring about a true redistribution of land tenure, nor can it bring about a redistribution of national income—which are the two primary objectives of true agrarian reform.

What defects and virtues do you find in the Colombian Institute for Agrarian Reform?

I think that I know INCORA well enough and it appears to be one of the organizations which, in relation to private enterprise, is the best run and most efficiently organized. I think that it has a team of young men with a great sense of patriotism who are dedicating their work, their energy, and their intelligence to this job which, as I said before, is agricultural fomentation. I feel that it will create a series of infrastructures that are important to the country.

The great fault I find in the Institute is that it has not been sufficiently concerned with the education of the country-dwellers. Not so much in the formal sense, since it has built schools and some cooperatives, but in the informal sense of giving them a consciousness and organization, so that in the future they may be able to form a large pressure group capable of changing this pseudo-agrarian reform into a true agrarian reform undertaken by the country-dwellers themselves.

In Putumayo, especially in the area of Sibundoy, plans for agrarian reform have encountered obstacles because of the opposition of a religious community. You are a sociologist and priest. From what point of view do you analyze the problem?

According to the information I have, since unfortunately I am not aware of the situation first-hand, it seems to be a classical case of the Church yielding to the temptation of political and economic power. It is not that the missionary fathers have too much land, although they do. But I think that fundamentally they are opposed to the intervention of INCORA because they feel that they may lose political power, that is to say they think they will lose control over the natives of the area, whom they are organizing into a type of theocracy.

This has happened in many places where there was communal action. For example, in the case of Tunjuelito I think that the idea that influence would be lost was totally contradicted when the promotion of private initiative and other institutions favoring the faithful of a determined community were permitted.

Many parish priests have opposed communal action as they are opposed to the agrarian reform, and they make themselves more unpopular. And I think that the missionary fathers are going to make themselves more unpopular if they continue to oppose it. Perhaps not in the short run and perhaps not in an apparent way, but I think that the natives will someday understand that they are being deprived of a great benefit, and that this is being done in a totally sectarian spirit. For that reason I think that, if the parish priests were to integrate themselves and attempt to promote agrarian reform, and if the missionary fathers were to become the standard-bearers of the agrarian reform and of INCORA in Sibundoy, both in the short and long run all these things would bring them great popularity and great influence. An influence that would not be paternalistic but truly democratic.

If the revolution were brought about by force, would you be partisan to the expropriation of Church property?

I am partisan to the expropriation of Church property even in the case that no revolution might occur.

XIX.
LAICIZATION

When circumstances impede men from devoting themselves to Christ, the priest's proper duty is to combat these circumstances, even at the cost of his being able to celebrate the eucharistic rite, which has no meaning without the devotion of Christians.

In the present structure of the Church it has been impossible for me to continue my priestly duties in the aspects of external cult. However, the Christian priesthood does not consist only of the celebration of external rites. The Mass, which is the final object of the priestly action, is fundamentally a communal action. But the Christian community cannot offer the sacrifice in an authentic form if it has not first fulfilled in an effective manner the precept of "love of thy neighbor."

I chose Christianity because I felt that in it I had found the best way of serving my neighbor. I was elected by Christ to be a priest forever, motivated by the desire to devote myself fulltime to loving my fellow man.

As a sociologist I wished this love to become effective through science and technique. Upon analyzing Colombian society I realized the need for a revolution that would give food to the hungry, drink to the thirsty, clothing to the naked, and bring about the well-being of the majorities in our country.

I feel that the revolutionary struggle is a Christian and priestly struggle. Only through this, given the concrete circumstances of our country, can we fulfill the love that men should have for their neighbors.

Ever since I became a priest I have tried all means possible to get laymen, Catholics and non-Catholics, to join the revolutionary struggle. In the absence of a massive response from the people to the action of the laymen, I have resolved to dedicate myself, fulfilling in this way part of my task of leading men through mutual love to the love of God. I consider this an essential duty of my Christian and priestly life as a Colombian. Notwithstanding that it is a task which at present conflicts with the discipline of the Church today.

I do not wish to be unfaithful to this discipline, nor do I wish to betray my conscience. For this reason I have asked the Cardinal to free me of my clerical obligations so that I may serve the people in the secular world. I sacrifice one of the rights that I love most dearly—to be able to celebrate the external rite of the Church as a priest—in order to create the conditions that make the cult more authentic.

I believe that my obligation with my fellow man to effectively fulfill the precept of "love thy neighbor" forces this sacrifice on me. The ultimate criterion of human decisions must be charity, must be supernatural love. I will run all the risks that this criterion demands of me.

XX.
CROSSROADS OF THE CHURCH
IN LATIN AMERICA

1. The Strength or Weakness of the Church?

It is a dilemma which presents itself to any foreign observer in Latin America and even to the Latin Americans themselves. When we fly over our cities we see them bristling with domes. We land and see the interiors of the different Catholic churches in every tourist's guide of the continent. In every town and in almost every village we see the "dear fathers," as the simple folk call them; the "curates" that we see in the city. The bishop, archbishop, or cardinal is without doubt one of the higher authorities.

The experience of the priest who travels through Latin America is also significant. There are many differences in almost all areas. Between workers and intellectuals there is generally open hostility. There is no meeting half way. However, throughout history we find some curious things. In nearly every country during the nineteenth or early twentieth centuries, there was confiscation of Church property and legislation passed which opposed what the hierarchy felt to be the interests of the Institution. It was difficult for a priest to continue teaching in a college or university of the State. I do not think that there is a country in Latin America where churches have not been burned or "curates" persecuted. When we manage to talk privately with Latin American Catholics, even with the more devoted, most of them say that they are anti-clerical and that they are displeased with the priests.

What then is the matter with the Latin American Church?

2. The Church of Cult and the Church of Faith

It has often been said that our Catholics are fetishists. It may well be that there are many manifestations of it. It is certainly evident in the preaching and teaching of Christian morality, with its emphasis on sexual matters and its insistence upon external observance. Some people maliciously insinuate that that is what brings the priests most money. However, there are many popular external practices, not specifically Christian, perhaps fetishistic, which do not represent any type of profit for the priests and yet the priests insist on them. As heirs of Spanish Catholicism we place emphasis on the external. It can be practiced more easily and widely.

The Spanish evangelization began and continued on a wide scale. In the midst of the era of Counter-Reform the scholastic catechisms were still being used. These were full of incomprehensible formulas, which the Indians were made to learn so that they could qualify quickly for the rite of baptism and thus conduct themselves in the consciousness of being good "apostles of Christ."

The Spanish Crown was cautious. It was aware of the influence of the clergy and so hindered the formation of an indigenous one. By the time it won independence from Spain, Latin America had been evangelized widely but not deeply. There were many baptized but few Christian consciences. Moreover, the shortage of clergy, caused by the emigration of Spanish priests, aggravated the situation. The Latin American Church continued to be a Church of external cult and not of Christian faith. Even today when the workers are asked: "What is the Holy Trinity?", they almost always reply firmly: "The Mother of Our Lord Jesus Christ."

3. The Church of Charity
and the Church of Faith

However, we Latin Americans do love. Not always in a rational
or constructive way. Nevertheless, there is love, cooperation,
hospitality, a spirit of service among our people. In the upper
class it is different. At the risk of generalizing too freely, it can
be said that those who brag most of their faith and their clericalism are the ones who love their neighbors least, and those who
really serve their brothers are often the ones who do not practice
the external cult of the Church. "Everything isn't as it appears,
nor does it appear as it is." The identification as "Christian" is
made in relation to the practice of love. When they speak of
"Catholic," people refer to the external practice. The Church
appears to be made up of a majority who practice but do not
know their faith and a minority who know their faith but do
not practice it, except externally. Can this be said to be Christian? In those who are of bad faith, in no way is it Christian.
In those who love, even when they are fetishists, if they are of
good faith, even when they believe that they are atheists, it is
certainly Christian. They belong to the soul of the Church, and
if they are baptized, they belong also to the body of the Church.

It appears to be totally anomalous: those who have faith do not
love, and those who love do not have faith—at least in the
explicit sense of the word.

4. The Witness of Charity

"He who loves fulfills the law," says St. Paul. "Love and do what
you will," says St. Augustine. The surest sign of predestination
is love of neighbor. St. John tells us: "If someone says he loves
God, whom he does not see, and does not love his neighbor
whom he does see, he is a liar."

However, this love for our neighbor must be effective. We will
not be judged only by our good intentions, but mainly by our

actions in favor of Christ represented in each one of our neighbors. "I was hungry and you did not give me to eat, I was thirsty and you did not give me to drink."

Under the present circumstances in Latin America we see that we cannot feed, or clothe, or house the majorities. Those who hold power constitute an economic minority which dominates political, cultural, and military power, and unfortunately also, ecclesiastical power in the countries in which the Church has temporal goods. This minority will not make decisions opposed to its own interests. For this reason governmental decisions are not made to benefit the majorities. In order to give them food, drink, and clothing, basic decisions are necessary, decisions which can only come from the government. Technical solutions we have or we can obtain. But who decides on their application? The minority, against its own interests? It is a sociological absurdity that a group would act against its own interests. The power must be taken for the majorities' part so that structural, economic, social, and political reforms benefiting these majorities may be realized. This is called revolution, and if it is necessary in order to fulfill love for one's neighbor, then it is necessary for a Christian to be revolutionary.

How difficult it is for those who are known as Catholics to understand this! How easy it is to understand this attitude if we consider our previous reflections upon the Church. Christians, Catholics, seem to be stoic spectators of the fall of the world, the world which they abhor. They do not join the struggle. They believe that in the words "my kingdom is not of this world" "world" means "present life" and not "sinful life," as it really does. They forget the prayer of Christ to the Father: "I do not ask that you remove them from the world but that you preserve them from evil." Often we become detached from the world but do not preserve ourselves from evil.

To the degree that the community loves is the eucharistic sacrifice which the priest offers authentic. This is not an individual but a collective offering. If there is no love between those who offer it, there should be no offering to God. Thus if the laity do not join the struggle for the well-being of their brothers, the priesthood tends to become ritualistic, individualistic, and superficial. The priest is under the obligation to assist the laity in their temporal responsibilities if this is what love demands. When this love appears no longer to be considered as patrimony of the Church, it is necessary to give firm witness that the community of the communal Church consists in charity. Unfortunately, the witness of the laity is still not identified in public opinion with the witness of the Church. The priest in this case must give witness so that public opinion is formed and shown that the witness of all the baptized is the witness of the Church.

To see a priest mixed up in politics and abandoning the external exercise of his priesthood is repulsive to our traditional mentality. However, we think that perhaps there may exist reasons, concerning love of one's neighbor and witness, that are truly priestly and that give impetus to this compromise in order to follow one's own conscience and, therefore, God.

When Christians live basically for love and to make others love, when the faith is a faith inspired in life and especially in the life of God, of Jesus, and of the Church, when the external rite is the true expression of love within the Christian community, we will be able to say that the Church is strong, without economic or political power but with charity.

If the temporal involvement of a priest in political struggles contributes to this, it seems that his sacrifice can be justified.

XXI.
THE UNITED FRONT

1. Why I Am Not Going to the Elections

The platform of the United Front of the Colombian people has no definition concerning the electoral struggle as a revolutionary tactic. In order to bring about the union of the revolutionaries we must insist on anything that will help unite us and avoid anything that will help separate us. If the electoral problem is an obstacle to this union, it is better not to undertake it, especially when we are still not sure that the elections will take place.

If I were partisan to the elections, the most logical thing to do would be to present a slate and enter myself as a candidate. In my opinion this would be to form a new group which would even further divide the opposition. This attitude would hinder me from accomplishing the resolved task of uniting the Colombian popular class.

I do not consider myself the representative of the Colombian popular class, or head of the United Front, or leader of the Colombian Revolution, because I was not elected by the people. I want to be accepted by them as a servant of the Revolution.

While the United Front is choosing its leaders, I am not a leader of the United Front, except in those cases where the members so determine. Since I am not going to participate in the elections, I must explain the motives that led me to this decision. Besides the reason given earlier (that of not dividing the opposition further) there are the following:

1. Under the present voting system the Colombian people must choose between Liberal and Conservative. Anything which divides the people is against their interests.

2. The electoral apparatus is in the hands of the oligarchy and for this reason "who counts votes, elects." The elections are determined more in the offices of the oligarchical government than in the voting booths.

3. Since it is impossible to beat those who control the electoral machinery and all the elements of power, the opposition groups who get into Parliament will never bring about revolutionary changes. On the contrary, their presence in Parliament makes it easier for the oligarchy to say that in Colombia there is democracy because there is opposition.

4. It does not seem to me to be good revolutionary education to tell the people in words to distrust the oligarchy on the one hand, and on the other to tell them in actions to hand over to the system something as precious to a man as is his political opinion.

5. I think that the time and money spent in drawing up a slate, discussing revenues, supplements, and leaders could be used to organize and unify the popular class at the bottom.

6. Should the miracle ever happen that the oligarchy makes a mistake in counting the ballots and the opposition became the majority (for example, in the case of a new plebiscite), we know that, as in Argentina with the triumph of Peronism, the oligarchy could annul the elections and stage a coup. An oligarchy which has no qualms about murdering revolutionary leaders, throwing the country into violence, and supporting a military regime is not going to hand over power merely because the opposition has won a majority of votes. And as we have already shown, it is virtually impossible to win such a majority.

Personally, I am in favor not of passive electoral abstention but of active, aggressive, revolutionary abstention. Active because it will be the manifestation of a rejection of the system, including the elections as a cog within that wheel; for this one must be politically motivated. Aggressive because the revolutionary commands will receive precise assignments on how to behave at the elections. Revolutionary because it will be used to unify and organize the popular class for a definitive assault on power.

2. Message to the Christians

The convulsions caused by the recent political, religious, and social events have possibly left the Christians in Colombia in a state of confusion. In these decisive moments of our history we Christians must be firm in the essential bases of our religion.

What is essential in Catholicism is love of neighbor. "He who loves his neighbor has fulfilled the law" (Rom. 13, 8). For this love to be real it must seek to be effective. If kindness, alms, the few free schools, the few housing plans, so-called "charity," does not feed the majority of the hungry, or clothe the majority of the naked, or teach the majority of the uneducated, we must seek effective means for achieving the well-being of the majorities.

The privileged minorities who hold power are not going to seek them, for generally the means would demand that the minorities sacrifice their privileges. For example, to create more jobs in Colombia capital should not be withdrawn in dollar form, but should be invested in the country. However, since the Colombian peso is devaluing every day, those who have money and power will never prohibit the exportation of money, because in exporting it they escape the effects of devaluation. It is necessary, then, to take the power from the privileged minority and give it to the poor majority. This, if done quickly, is the essential element of a revolution. The Revolution can be peaceful if the minorities put up no violent resistance.

The Revolution is the means of obtaining a government that will feed the hungry, clothe the naked, teach the uneducated, perform works of charity, love their neighbors not only in a transitory and occasional way, not just a few but the majority of their neighbors. For this reason the Revolution is not only permissible but obligatory for Christians who see in it the one effective and complete way to create love for all.

It is certain that "there is no law but God's law" (Rom. 13, 1). But St. Thomas says that concrete attribution of authority is made by the people. When there is an authority opposed to the

172

people, this authority is illegitimate and tyrannical. We Christians can and must fight against tyranny. The present government is tyrannical because it supports only twenty percent of the electors and because its decisions stem from the privileged minorities.

The temporal defects of the Church should not scandalize us, for the Church is human. What is important is to believe that it is also divine and that if we Christians comply with our obligation to love our neighbor, we are strengthening the Church.

I have given up the duties and privileges of the clergy but I have not ceased to be a priest. I believe that I joined the Revolution out of love of my neighbor. I have stopped saying Mass in order to fulfill this love of neighbor in the temporal, economic, and social world. When my neighbor no longer holds anything against me, when the Revolution has been completed, I will return to offering Mass, God permitting. I think that in this way I follow Christ's injunction: "If you bring your offering to the altar and there you remember that your brother has something against you, leave your offering there and go; first make peace with your brother, and then come and present your offering" (Mt. 5, 23–24). After the Revolution we Christians will be aware that we are establishing a system which is oriented towards the love of our neighbor. The struggle is long; let us begin now.

3. Message to the Communists

Because of the traditional relationship between Christians and Marxists, between the Church and the Communist Party, suspicions and erroneous suppositions could arise with respect to the relationship established in the United Front between Christians and Marxists and between a priest and the Communist Party. For this reason, I think it necessary that my relationship with the Communist Party and its position within the United Front remain quite clear to the Colombian people.

I have said that, as a Colombian, as a sociologist, as a Christian, and as a priest, I am a revolutionary. I feel that the Communist Party has elements that are authentically revolutionary and because of that I cannot, either as a Colombian, or as a sociologist, or as a Christian, or as a priest, be anti-Communist. I am not anti-Communist as a Colombian because anti-Communism is oriented towards persecuting non-conformist compatriots, Communist or not, of whom the majority are the poor. I am not anti-Communist as a sociologist because in the Communist plan of fighting poverty, hunger, illiteracy, lack of housing and services for the people, effective and scientific solutions are to be found. I am not anti-Communist as a Christian because I believe that anti-Communism makes a blanket condemnation of everything Communists defend, and there are both just and unjust things in what they defend. In condemning them all we are condemning the just and the unjust equally, and this is anti-Christian. I am not anti-Communist as a priest because even though the Communists themselves do not know it, there are many among them who are truly Christian. If they are of good faith, they can have sanctifying grace; and if they have sanctifying grace and love their neighbor, they will be saved. My role as a priest, even though I do not exercise the external rite, is to try to lead men to God, and the most effective way to do this is to lead men to serve their neighbors according to their consciences.

I have no intention of proselytizing my Communist brothers, trying to get them to accept the dogma and to practice the cult of the Church. But this I am certainly working towards, that all men act according to their conscience, sincerely seek the truth, and love their neighbor in an effective way. The Communists must well know that I will not join their ranks, that I am not, nor will I be a Communist, either as a Colombian, or as a sociologist, or as a Christian, or as a priest. However, I am ready to fight alongside them for common goals: opposing the oligarchy and the domination of the United States, in order to take power for the popular class.

I do not want the public to identify me with the Communists, and for this reason I have always made it a point to appear in the company not only of the Communists but of all the other revolutionaries.

It is not important that the press insists on presenting me as a Communist. I prefer to follow my conscience than to bend under pressure from the oligarchy. I prefer to follow the norms of the pontiffs of the Church before those of the pontiffs of our ruling class. John XXIII authorizes me to join in a unity of action with the Communists when he says in his encyclical *Pacem in Terris:*

One must also carefully distinguish between the philosophical theories concerning the nature, the origin, and the end of the world and of man, and the initiatives of the economic, social, cultural, or political order, however much such initiatives have been originated and inspired in these philosophical theories; because the doctrines, once elaborated and defined, no longer change, whereas such initiatives encountered in continually changing historical situations are necessarily subject to the same changes. Moreover, who can deny that, in the dictates of right reason and the interpretations of the just aspirations of man, there can be good elements worthy of approbation?

Accordingly, it may sometimes happen that certain contacts in the political order which heretofore were considered entirely useless, today may on the contrary be advantageous, or could become so. Whether or not such a moment has arrived, and the form and degree to which these contacts may be realized with regard to obtaining positive ends, whether in the economic or social field, or in the cultural or political field—these are points which can only be shown by the virtue of prudence, the governor of all the virtues which rule the individual and social moral life.

When the popular class takes power, thanks to the collaboration of all the revolutionaries, our people will discuss their religious orientation.

The example of Poland shows us that Socialism can be built without destroying the essentials of Christianity. As a Polish priest said: "We Christians have an obligation to contribute to the construction of the Socialist State always and when we are permitted to adore God as we wish."

4. Assignments

Let us consider as the principle objective of the revolutionary struggle the union and the organization of the Colombian popular class in order to take power.

Let us found this union in the spirit and along the general lines of the platform of the United Front of the People.

Let us sponsor a popular organization structured from the bottom up: from neighborhood to town, from suburb to center, from countryside to city. To do this the Colombian popular class must be organized into groups of five or ten, with no distinction between partisan or opposition movements and the non-aligned in these groups and movements, with the sole condition that they accept the general lines of the platform of the United Front of the People.

The first assignment for these commands of the United Front will be the discussion and dissemination of the platform. This platform has not been given to Colombians as a dogma or as a definitive program. It is a proposal to be examined by the Colombian popular class, so that they may discuss it, change it, and amplify it, since that is what is to be applied when this class takes power.

The second assignment is to disseminate the platform by every media: sending it out printed, mimeographed, typewritten, hand-written, reading it to illiterate compatriots, shouting it in the fields and streets of Colombia.

The third assignment is to organize the distribution and financing of the newspaper *Frente Unido*. The oligarchy will not support a publication which is destined to clash with them. In a revolutionary newspaper the numerous small contributions of the poor are more important than the suspect and adulterated donations of the rich.

The newspaper costs one peso: a peso a week for the Revolution—something less than the cost of a beer—, which will be put towards not only the financing of the newspaper but also the support of the minimum political apparatus necessary to take power for the popular class. The *Frente Unido* will be the thread which unifies the popular commands and creates a large net supporting the entire organization of the working and farming classes.

The fourth assignment will be the election of command leaders, and the formation of farm commands, factory commands, neighborhood commands, district, municipal, and departmental commands, so that at the end of the year we can call a large popular convention in Bogotá to elect a national command of the Revolution and determine the tactics to be followed in the definitive assault for power.

The most powerful, the richest, the best educated, the better families, the local bosses and traditional leaders need not attend this convention. Those who do attend will be the weak, the ignorant, the imprudent—according to the oligarchy—, the poor, the hungry, the ill-clothed, but the ones who hold the ideals of the Revolution and have the flame of struggle for their brothers in their hearts and in their arms.

By then the municipal, regional, and departmental commands which will have been elected will be provisional commands. All Colombians, without discrimination, will participate in them. They may be representatives of worker, farmer, or student societies or they may be from among the non-aligned. In the provisional commands of the United Front no one will be judged by what he represents but by what he does for the Revolution. For now effectiveness in the organization will be proved with assignments emanating from the provisional committee which functions at the national level.

When the national command of the United Front is established, as a result of the Bogotá convention, it will give the revolutionary assignments and determine the tactical steps towards the take-over of power by the popular class.

The take-over may be sudden or progressive. It all depends on the unity and organization of the popular class on the one hand, and on the belligerent or non-belligerent attitude of the oligarchy on the other. The popular class has not decided on the way to take power; it has decided that it has to be taken sooner or later. It is the oligarchy who must decide how the power is going to be given over. If it is given over peacefully, the popular class will take it peacefully. If they do not want to give it up without a struggle, the popular class will take it with a struggle.

For the union of the popular class, unto death.

For the organization of the popular class, unto death.

For the take-over of power for the popular class, unto death.

5. Message to the Military

After having seen the power of forty armed and disciplined men over a crowd of four thousand in the city of Girardot, I decided to make a fervent call to the armed forces of Colombia to become aware of the historic moment in which we are living, and to decide for themselves now how they will participate in the revolutionary struggle.

On various occasions I have seen uniformed men—farmers and workers, never elements of the ruling class—fighting and persecuting farmers, workers, and students who represent the majority of Colombians. And it is with rare exception that I have found members of the oligarchy among the officials and subofficials. Anyone who considers the contrast between the Colombian majorities clamoring for revolution and the small military minorities repressing the people in order to protect a few small privileged families must ask himself what reasons induce these elements of the people to persecute their fellows.

It could not be for the economic advantages. All military personnel are poorly paid. The military are generally not permitted to study for a life outside the army. When they reach higher rank, they try to buy a corner house to open a store to support them in their retirement. I have seen generals and colonels apply for posts as teachers of physical education in high schools and as insurance salesmen. The salary for personnel on active duty is low, but it is even lower for retired personnel. They receive no medical attention or any other economic benefits. However, we know that a third of our national budget goes to the armed forces. As is obvious, the war budget is not used to pay the Colombian military but to buy the scrap metal the United States sells us, to maintain the material elements, and to support internal repression in which Colombians kill their own brothers.

It may be that the motive behind what the military does is devotion to the Fatherland, the Constitution, and the laws. But the Colombian Fatherland consists mainly in its men, and the majority of these are suffering and cut off from power. The Constitution is constantly violated in that jobs, property, freedom, and participation in power are not given to the people who ought to be, according to the Constitution, the ones to decide public policy in the country. The Constitution is violated when martial law is maintained after the causes that were the pretext for its declaration have ceased. The laws are violated when citizens are detained without a warrant for arrest, when the mail is withheld, when curfews are imposed, when the telephones are tapped, and lies and tricks are used to persecute the revolutionaries.

Perhaps it is necessary to better inform the military about the Fatherland, the Constitution, and the laws, so that they do not think that the Fatherland consists in the twenty-four families whom they actually protect, for whom they spill their blood, and from whom they receive such poor remuneration.

Perhaps the principal reason that the military continues to be the armed extension of the oligarchy is the lack of opportunity in other fields of human activity which exists in Colombia. The military should understand that when the Revolution triumphs, the economy will be planned, schools, colleges, and universities will be open to all Colombians, and not only they but their sons too will have the opportunity for remunerative employment and unrestricted careers. While it lasts the reactionary enemy will have an army, not for the defense of the privileged

179

minorities, but for the defense of the people. The sacrifices made then will be made to develop the Fatherland, not destroy it.

The honor of the army will not then be stained by the caprice of the oligarchy and of their lackeys who have the armed forces at their service. We will no longer see three-star generals made destitute for having talked of structural reform and pressure groups. We will no longer see generals who are from the middle class accused of being contrabandists in public scandals while their superiors in the upper class or connected with the Colombian oligarchy engage in contraband activities which they manage to keep secret, activities which are more directly detrimental to the interests of the country and national sovereignty.

Military men: the United Front promises you to unify the popular class and to organize them to take power. Do not fail to join us on the field of battle where we will strike the fatal blow against this oligarchy that oppresses all Colombians, that oppresses you as it oppresses us.

6. Message to the Non-Aligned

The symptoms of laxity and putrefaction in the National Front are common to those of all degenerating regimes in the final stages of their existence. The leaders drown in parties and orgies the unrest that popular ferment produces in them, and devote political activity to caucuses and internal struggles between anachronistic and unpopular directories.

The disputes between the Llerases, the Gomezes, the Ospinases, and the other families of our feudal aristocracy no longer interest the people. The people are hungry. They are dissatisfied. They have decided to unite and organize themselves. The people above all have made the unswerving decision to take power.

In past elections there was still no need for the oligarchy to invent votes; if we permit the next elections to take place, then they will certainly have to invent many votes. The abstentionists constitute the majority of the electors. Seventy percent of the

Colombians did not go to the polls. Anyone having an elemental knowledge of the Colombian people, anyone who has attended the popular meetings with me must have come to the conclusion that the abstentionists are opposed to the National Front and the oligarchy.

In general, those who abstain are those revolutionaries who are not organized into political groups. The revolutionary and anti-partisan spirit that the political groups which have entered the United Front have shown has allowed them to obtain a greater number of adherents. Most Colombians have joined the United Front without joining the already existent political groups. These groups have to understand that the principle activity of the United Front ought to be the organization of the non-aligned.

The non-aligned must be organized from the bottom up, with its own leaders and strong but non-dictatorial authority. At present, the main link between them is the platform of the United Front of the People which I have presented as a proposal to the Colombian popular class. It is possible that my name still holds too much importance in this group. At an initial stage, while my name serves to stimulate agitation and revolutionary organization, it can be quite useful. It would be infantile to repeat the same mistakes that produced the calamities of earlier revolutionary movements. We have already seen how the oligarchy assassinated Jorge Eliécer Gaitán. We have already seen how the reaction of the people at this moment was not to regroup themselves around the revolutionary leaders but to run to the leaders of the oligarchy who arrived at the presidential palace on the shoulders of the people to betray the revolutionary movement. We have already seen how these disorganized people wanted to fight in the cities where the enemy is stronger. We have already seen how the people allowed themselves to become disconcerted and began burning and looting instead of retreating to the countryside where the enemy is weaker and where the revolutionaries have greater resources.

We are running a race with the oligarchy. It is possible that they will assassinate me before a solid organization of the non-aligned can be formed. I think it would be too slow for them to jail me or invent a propaganda trial. So I think assassination is more likely. What is important is that the Colombian people have precise assignments should this happen.

The first is to retreat to the country, not fight in the city. The second is to take no offensive action as long as there is no rural organization capable of maintaining it. It is also necessary for the non-aligned to take note of the seriousness of this moment and of their historical responsibility. Each minute that we lose in organization is a minute's advantage for the oligarchy.

The many demonstrations, the enthusiasm, and the revolutionary agitation are useful insofar as they reflect immediately upon a grass-roots organization. It is necessary that each simple farmer, each common worker, and each revolutionary feel responsible for forming a command of the United Front with a few co-workers or friends, without waiting for directives and without awaiting orders. They must unite:

1. To discuss and disseminate the platform of the United Front.
2. To distribute and finance the newspaper *Frente Unido*.
3. To carry out the immediate assignments of operations.
4. To coordinate with the other basic commands in order to form commands on the factory, college or university, neighborhood, district, municipal, regional, and departmental levels.
5. To prepare the delegates for the people's national convention, to be held on the 11th or 12th of December 1965.

The demonstration on October 10th at 5 o'clock in the Plaza de Bolívar will be the occasion for the non-aligned to present themselves in organized commands and societies. In this demonstration the Colombian people and especially those from the capital will protest against the state of martial law and all of its repressive consequences against the Colombian people: the union persecution, the persecution of the leaders of the opposition, the new taxes, the latest devaluation, and so forth.

Electoral abstention alone is not a weapon of revolutionary combat. It must be led by an organization and by an aggressive and active discipline. The non-aligned, the non-partisan revolutionaries, will have to transform themselves from a weak, amorphous mass into a battering ram that will not stop battering at the system until the system has totally crumbled.

7. Message to the Trade Unions

Few groups in Colombia have such a tradition of struggle and organization as do the workers, the urban laborers. In spite of the fact that the industrialization of Colombia did not become important nationally until 1939, Colombian unionism, both rural and urban, has a tradition of struggle dating back before this time. The riots of the banana workers are evidence of this struggle. The government of Alfonso López marked an important stage in labor organization and in the Colombian union struggle. Unionism surged as an aggressive and independent force, but soon, under reactionary governments, it began to pall under paternalistic and imperialistic elements and with strikebreakers selling out to the government. Our ruling class has succeeded in dividing the working class, and after debilitating it on religious and political pretexts, as it had already weakened the popular class, it resolved at the Cartagena Congress to purge it of Communist elements, in other words, to remove all elements not submitting to national and North American patronization.

However, the pressure of the system was common to all workers. Gaitán's movement consolidated a class consciousness that official violence has not been able to blot out in the nineteen years it has been in existence. The mercenary leaders, selling out to the oligarchy, behave more impudently each time, and have to use more and more arbitrary and violent measures to maintain power.

The National Front is accelerating the social struggle in Colombia by instituting itself as the first class party in Colombia, a party of the privileged class which consolidates the union of oppressors against the oppressed, challenging the Colombian popular class to constitute, according to the advice of José Antonio Galán, "the union of the oppressed against the oppressors."

The government of the National Front brought about three devaluations, increased by two hundred percent public and war expenditures, and tried to repair the serious fiscal failure by imposing on the Colombian people a sales tax, a gasoline tax, and a "pound cake tax." The national walk-out of January twenty-fifth was the culmination of a social ferment which was sold out to the oligarchy so that they could make a pound cake which they themselves would have to eat. However, the system is so disintegrated and corrupt that the Parliamentary political machine did not function either for the pound cake or extraordinary power.

Then dictatorship was re-established. They availed themselves of a student strike to declare martial law, which is still in effect, contrary to the Constitution, to legislate on economic matters, and to bring about labor demagogy. The most serious thing about the present system is that not only are the workers discontent, but the oligarchy is as well, and I say most serious because when the oligarchy is discontent the possibility of a coup becomes more immediate.

When political equipment fails, the oligarchy turns to military equipment. The military government which is now in power may possibly awaken hopes through demagogic measures. Lately, our people have unanimously cried for revolution. However, we still lack sufficient consciousness and adequate organization to oppose the deceit that will predominate the demagogic measures after the fall of the hated government of the National Front.

An interminable series of legal and illegal strikes have been begun in our country. All these struggles or successes strengthen the revolutionary movement because they unify, organize, and consolidate the consciousness of the Colombian working class. The members of all the union locals are unified, together with many of their leaders, around the platform of the United Front of the People. The workers together with the students constitute the bastion capable of opposing the new forms of deceit that the oligarchy will adopt. Above all, it is necessary that the workers decide to use their relative financial capability and their unquestionable organizational capability in the revolutionary struggle and in the organization of the rest of the Colombian popular class.

It has been said that the unionists are the oligarchy of the popular class. I do not think so. Because of the exploitive attitude of the oligarchy, even those union men—many of them at least—who work in monopolistic businesses, and therefore benefit from a number of the privileges which these businesses have, adopted a frankly revanchist and revolutionary attitude.

The Colombian working class must, in these crucial moments of our history, dedicate their efforts towards the unity and organization of the Colombian popular class in order to take power. Through each struggle for immediate advantage the people must not lose sight of the fact that the total and definitive labor recovery will only come as a result of the taking of power by the majorities, the Colombian popular classes. The unity, organization, and struggle for this definitive recovery depend on the unity, organization, and capacity to fight for present recovery. The union leaders who are afraid of the dissemination of the platform of the United Front are the ones who fear unity because they know that a united and organized working class would rigorously collect whatever they have paid to the national and foreign ruling classes.

The working class, like the Colombian people, has in many cases been superior to its leaders. When the working class unites from below it will constitute the pressure necessary for the Colombian people to oust the leaders who do not want union or revolution, as though a torrent had swept through.

8. Father Torres Speaks

The Cardinal reduced me to the lay state by a decree in which he says that this reduction will be in accord with an order from Rome. This order has not arrived, for they told me that they asked the Cardinal to speak with me before imposing laical sanction on me and he did not heed this order.

Unfortunately, the Cardinal gives the impression of continuing in the same key: neither explaining nor proving in what way I am opposed to the Catholic Church. It seems that he is acting under pressure from the groups which have subjugated the country.

The public statements of his Eminence the Cardinal contradict his private statements. When I spoke with him personally we saw that the only way to keep our consciences clear was for me to ask for a reduction to lay status. He told me that it was a painful decision for him but that he hoped that when I considered it convenient I would return to the exercise of my priesthood and that he would receive me with open arms.

9. Message to the Peasants

According to the census the rural population has decreased. However, the census considers urban any area with more than 1500 inhabitants. In reality this is not so. We can say that the majority of the Colombian population is rural.

Besides numbers, the most important fact is that the rural Colombians contribute the most to the national income. Ninety percent of the exports are agricultural (coffee, bananas, tobacco, sugar). Without agriculture we would not be able to import machines or the food we lack. Unfortunately, as with everything else in this system, the contribution of the peasants benefits only a few. The profits are concentrated in the hands of those who run the associations (of coffee producers, cotton growers, United Fruit, banana growers, and tobacco growers) and the banks (especially the Bank of the Republic). The portion of the profits which the government receives are used in so-called "operating costs," that is, to pay employees (whose numbers have been doubled because of the duplication needed to preserve parity of the parties in governmental administration) and for purchasing old arms to kill the peasants who have made the money to purchase them.

The contrast between the economic and social importance of the peasants and the treatment they receive is clearly scandalous. The violence has been principally rural. It is the government that began it in 1947, first using the police and then, since 1948, using the army.

The Liberal oligarchy paid the Liberal peasants and the Conservative oligarchy paid the Conservative peasants for the peasants to kill their own people. The oligarchy came out without a scratch. And when the oligarchy no longer needed them, they declared them bandits, had them hunted down like wild beasts, and then published the photographs of their bodies on the front page of the newspaper, boasting of their triumph in the name of peace, justice, and legality.

This governmental violence financed by the oligarchy later taught the peasants many things. It taught them to recognize their true enemy in the oligarchy. It taught them to run first, defend themselves later. It taught them to attack in order to obtain what the oligarchy obtained through violence—farms, crops, livestock, power. The system did not give them these things. On the contrary, the peasants have the lowest salaries, the fewest schools, the worst housing, and the fewest possibilities for progress.

When they had killed the known ringleaders, the government forces burned the areas controlled by these peasants. With the United States advising a cut-back, the leaders of the Colombian government claimed that they could not allow "suspect" areas to be left unwatched, even though they may have been peaceful. The army had to increase its importance to show that its existence was necessary and thereby to increase its budget.

The government says that the peasants started the violence. The peasants say it was the government. In France intellectuals of every leaning, after having investigated, say that the peasants are right.

I wish to challenge the government to request, if it dares, that a United Nations investigatory commission, made up of neutral countries (for example, Egypt, India, and Chile), judge the cases of Marquetalia, Pato, Guayabero, and Río Chiquito.

We see that the landings of the Colombian army, led by the North American military mission in the "independent republics," are the image of the "Marine" landing in Santo Domingo. The landings will continue. Yesterday in Río Chiquito, tomorrow in Sumapaz, the day after tomorrow in the Ariari and the Llanos. The army begins with civic-military action and ends with bombardments, it begins showing its teeth and ends shooting bullets. The peasants now know that the army carries bread in its outstretched hand and a dagger in the hand held behind its back. The "dependent republic" of Colombia will continue to obey the North Americans in order to destroy by blood and fire the other republics of independent Colombians. The North American cabinet has so decreed. Our peasants know on what to rely. They now know what to prepare for. They do not rush into danger, but neither do they run away from the struggle.

Now the oligarchy, under martial law, has removed people from the public squares. It pursues them with machine guns even in closed districts, as in Medellín. When they make life impossible for us in the city, we must go to the country. And from the country we cannot cast ourselves into the sea. There we will have to resist. The peasants ought to prepare themselves

188

for this, by organizing the commandos of the United Front into groups of five or ten, ridding the area of traitors to the people's cause, preparing caches of food and clothing, readying for a prolonged struggle, stopping neither to provoke nor offer resistance when conditions are unfavorable to the people.

The oligarchy will continue to reaffirm the peasants in their conviction that they must support the revolutionary forces. Why have they not killed the guerrilla from Simacota? But for the support of the peasants. When the oligarchy leaves no other route, the peasants will have to give refuge to the urban revolutionaries, to the workers and students. For the moment you must unify and organize yourselves to prepare to undertake the final great struggle.

10. Organizing the Non-Aligned

The grass-roots union of the popular class is a simple matter. The hungry, the unemployed, the insecure, the poor, the uneducated identify themselves easily with concrete political objectives and especially with the main objective which is the seizing of power for the Colombian popular class.

The organization of the popular class has come about much more easily and quickly than it was thought. The organizational precedents left by the union, the cooperative, communal action, and so forth have helped. But the basic thing is the desire of the people to organize themselves. "Necessity is the mother of invention." The people have realized that organization is the basis of the revolutionary movement. For this reason they have succeeded in overcoming the feelings of inferiority, timidity, and apathy. The farmers and workers have begun to feel directly responsible for the Revolution and have therefore begun, without awaiting orders from above, to organize themselves into groups of three, five, ten, or more.

The organization of the grass-roots is a fact, and more and more of a fact each day. Among the leaders and intellectuals it is a different story. They are being cautious and thoughtful. But fortunately, while the "revolutionary intellectuals" are cudgeling their brains seeking "the exact formula" for the Colombian Revolution on the shelves of the libraries, the people have found this formula through their suffering and their awareness of being exploited, persecuted, and humiliated.

The United Front of the People is composed of the organized political movements that have approved the platform for struggle and of all Colombians (Liberals, Conservatives, Anapists, Lopists, the M.R.L., hard-liners, Communists expelled or not, organized or not, Christian Democrats, Nationalists, Independents, and so forth) who approve of this platform.

We need to unite the oppressed against the oppressors. But in Colombia the majority of the oppressed do not belong to organized political groups. They are the non-aligned who on the whole want the Revolution but are not organized.

What then is the principle duty of the revolutionaries who are more conscientious, more organized, and more aligned, not so much with their group but with the Colombian Revolution? It is to organize the non-aligned, to make them align themselves. And this must be the primary concern of the United Front. Is it necessary for them to become Christian Democrats, Communists, Emerrelists, or Anapists? Is not the main objective to have them align themselves with the Colombian Revolution? If they do not wish to join an already existent opposition group, are we going to prohibit them from taking part in the Revolution? By what right? By right of the majority? Not at all, because they are the majority. By right of being better prepared? This can only be judged on the basis of facts, not identification cards or declarations. History will be the judge. For now, let us have mutual respect, and rather than seek honor and high position in the revolutionary hierarchy, let us dedicate ourselves to the Revolution. Let us dedicate ourselves to organizing those who are not organized. Let us call them whatever they wish to be called: "Non-aligned," "Aligned with the United Front," "Revolutionaries." Although I do not approve of personality sway over and above all considerations of organization, if this is sub-ordinated to the ideal of the organization, we can accept it for now. If the people wish to be called "Camilists," then let them, on the condition that they organize. It is not a question of form-ing a new party or a new movement, but rather a new organiza-tion of the unorganized to get them to align themselves with the United Front and the Revolution. But let us not oblige them to adopt new titles if they do not wish to.

It is logical that "at high levels" differences arise. Let us not get too worked up over this; let us just get on with the Revolu-tion. The people will be the ones to decide on the name of the non-aligned. The people will decide if, in the future, they will form another party. For now the task is to convince them to form a new organization that will become part of the United Front. In the task of forming this organization all true revolu-tionaries and all members of the United Front of the People must join forces.

11. Message to the Women

Colombian women, like the women of all underdeveloped coun-tries, have always been in an inferior position in regard to men and society. These positions vary according to the standard of living of the people.

In the popular class the woman has many physical duties and almost no intellectual rights. The women of the popular class have the highest level of illiteracy. They must work without complaining and on occasion do the heavy work in and around the home (the garden, pigs, chickens, dogs, and so forth) with no consideration to the problems and responsibilities of mother-hood.

The working class woman enjoys no social and even less legal protection. When in a country like ours the husband, plagued by misery, unemployment, faced with the overwhelming re-sponsibilities of a large family, takes refuge in vice and abandons his family, the wife must bear the whole burden. How many workers' homes during working hours are found closed and padlocked, full of half-clothed and half-starved children waiting for their mother to return home so they may get something to eat.

The middle class woman is also exploited by men. It is possible that in this class relations with the husbands are more equalitarian. However, these families could not survive if the women did not work, and we know that the working woman, the office girl, suffers all types of exploitation and pressure from the boss.

The woman of the upper class must be relegated to leisure, to card games and social affairs, because of the lack of intellectual and professional opportunities in our society. In this class, marital fidelity is required only of the woman. Censorship falls only on her when she commits an error of this type. Although the law calls for equal rights and duties, in reality such equality does not exist.

In politics, the men of the popular class have been up to now led by the caprice of the oligarchy. Abstention has been the first cry of revolt of a whole class which has no faith in the fabulous tales of the ruling class. There are other signs of unification and organization among the discontent. However, the oligarchy, like an octopus, is beginning to extend its tentacles to the Colombian women. Men of this class have given them the right to vote in order to continue using them as instruments.

The Colombian woman is a human being, not a mere instrument. The Colombian wife is aware that she is being exploited not only by society, as are the majority of Colombians, but also by her husband. The Colombian woman has fighting discipline, has shown generosity in her sacrifices for others, and has greater resistance to physical pain. The Colombian woman, like all women, has more sentiment, more sensitivity, and more intuition. All these qualities must be praised and put to use, not for the oligarchy or for men as such, but for a revolutionary ideal converted into the ideal for women.

On the other hand, the woman has seen with more intuition perhaps how the men have been deceived by voting cards and minor party struggles. The Colombian woman is not infected with the egoistic temptation of power. The oligarchy wishes to infect her with it but it does not realize that, if Colombian men are naturally suspicious, the women are even more so. They know very well that the vote is the new form of exploitation which the oligarchy has invented. The Colombian woman is readying herself for the Revolution. She has been and will be the support of the revolutionary man. She has to be the heart of the Revolution. If every revolutionary has a home with a wife who supports, understands, and helps him, we will have many more men deciding to fight. After the Revolution, the wife will know that equality of rights and duties will not remain merely a dead letter, but that it will be a reality that she herself, as a popular and revolutionary force, will be able to guarantee.

The problems of divorce and birth control that the Colombian wife thinks can be solved within a conformist and oppressive system can only be solved under a regime which respects the conscience of individuals and individual, familial, and social rights. They can only be solved when the State has true autonomy and at the same time respect in relation to the ecclesiastical hierarchy.

The Colombian wife has sufficient generosity to be able to place her personal problems within the framework of a larger ideal where they will be resolved without neglecting the other needs of her fellow citizens. This ideal can be realized only by bringing about an authentic Colombian Revolution.

12. The Platform and the Revolution

The United Front of the People is the result of a number of years of experience and reflection. The intended union of the political opposition groups and the other dissatisfied Colombians had to face two main problems. The first is the lack of size and the second is the lack of a clear definition. The size could easily have been limited according to religious motives, traditional political motives, group or leader loyalties. It was necessary to build a union around concrete objectives which would unify all Colombians regardless of religious beliefs, party, group, or leader attachments. The platform of struggle of the United Front of the People can be realized only after the people have taken power. Its only novelty consists in its seeking of the common points pertaining to the Revolution without entering into religious or party differences. It can be accepted by Catholics and non-Catholics, by poor Liberals and poor Conservatives, by the revolutionary elements of the M.R.L., the Communist, Anapo, and Christian Democratic Parties, and especially by the revolutionary elements of the non-aligned in these groups. However, it is necessary to explain that this platform leans towards the establishment of a Socialist State, that is, "Socialist" understood only in a technical and positive sense and not to be confused with the ideological—practical, not theoretical Socialism.

When a revolutionary platform is talked about many experts become involved. However, when it is specified that the Revolution consist of a fundamental reorganization of the State through the application of science and technology to bring about reforms benefiting the majorities, many bow out.

The platform does not mention tactics for taking power. However, some feel, as does Dr. Alfonso López Michelsen, that this platform is not useful for an immediate electoral struggle, and moreover that the platform is becoming associated with the name of Camilo Torres and I have clearly given reasons why I will not run for election. Although these reasons may in no way justify any attack by me on the other opposition groups, revolutionary or not, in fact the electoral groups deviate from the platform on any excuse. On the other hand, the followers of the platform, when planning the take-over of political power as an indispensable condition for applying the platform, necessarily have to make a tactical decision: to follow through to the ultimate consequences and use whatever means the oligarchy leaves open to seize power. This attitude has no great ideological consequences because the Church itself has established the conditions for a just war. However, many "revolutionaries" in fact do not wish to follow through to the ultimate consequences.

A platform which plans a type of Socialist State and the liberation of Colombia from North American imperialism cannot be indifferent to the movements which lean towards Socialism and espouse liberation from imperialism. Even though these movements contain ideological elements that are discrepant in scientific, positive, and practical aspects, they are more akin to us. This solidarity in practice drives away many timid "revolutionaries" who are more insistent on ideology than on revolution.

There is one fact evident in the movement of the United Front and that is that it is a mass movement that has formed in little time. Thus many have recently joined. Their motives for joining differ. Some came to acquire an important position and left frustrated. Others thought a new party was being formed and so they left the way they came—very quickly. As the revolutionary line of the United Front becomes more and more definitive and aggressive, the "fellow travelers" of the Revolution will continue to fall by the wayside to return home or wait for the others to complete the Revolution and then join it.

The important thing is that the Colombian popular class continue to move forward, without a single step backwards, in spite of the defections, in spite of the rumors, in spite of the betrayals. The decision of the poor that they do not want their sons to accuse them in the future of having betrayed their historical and revolutionary vocation will be what determines the situation. They know that I will follow through to the ultimate consequences and that, if only a handful of determined men remain with me, then we will continue the struggle.

Although this is going to be a prolonged struggle, the important thing is that all who have decided to join us have also decided to stay with us to the end.

13. Message to Students

Students are a privileged group in any underdeveloped country. Poor nations pay a very high price for their few college and university graduates. In Colombia in particular, given the large number of private colleges and universities, the economic factor has been a determining factor in education. In a country where sixty percent are illiterate, eight percent have a bachelor's degree, and one percent are professionals, the students are one of the few groups equipped to analyze the Colombian situation in comparison to other situations and with regard to possible solutions.

Moreover, the university student—in the university where it is not a crime to hold an opinion and in the college where there is freedom of expression—has simultaneously two privileges: the power to ascend the social scale by means of academic grades, and the power to be non-conformist and rebellious without impeding this ascent. These advantages make the students a decisive element in the Latin American Revolution. During the agitational phase of the Revolution, student efforts were very effective. During the organizing phase, their efforts were secondary in Colombia. In the direct struggle, notwithstanding the honorable exceptions which have arisen in our revolutionary history, their role has not been a determining one either.

We know that agitation is important, but its true effect is lost if it is not followed by organization and the struggle for the power take-over. One of the main reasons why the involvement of the students in the Revolution is transitory and superficial is the lack of student involvement in the personal, family, and economic struggle.

The students' non-conformity tends to be emotional (sentimentalism or frustration) or purely intellectual. This also explains the fact that at the end of a university career the non-conformity disappears or at least is concealed, and the rebel students cease to be non-conformist in order to convert into bourgeois professionals who, to buy the status symbols of the

196

middle class, have to sell their consciences in exchange for a higher salary.

These circumstances can threaten the possibility for a mature and responsible reply by the students to the historic moment that Colombia is now going through. The economic and political crisis is making itself felt most on the workers and farmers. The student, generally isolated from these problems, could think that purely speculative or superficial revolutionary activity is enough. Their lack of awareness of the problems could make the students betray their historical vocation: that when the country needs their total involvement the students continue with words and good intentions but nothing more; that when the movement of the masses calls for daily and continuous work, the students comply with shouts, stone-throwing, and sporadic demonstrations; that when the popular class needs an effective, disciplined, and responsible presence in its ranks, the students reply with vain promises or excuses.

The revolutionary conviction of the students must carry them through to the very end. Poverty and persecution ought not to be sought out. But under the present system, they are the logical consequences of a fight against the prevailing structures. Under the present system they are the signs which attest a revolutionary life. Their conviction must bring the students to participate in the economic penury and social persecution of the workers and farmers. Then their involvement with the Revolution passes from theory into practice. If it is complete, it is irreversible; the professional cannot take a step backwards without a flagrant betrayal of his conscience, his people, and his historic calling.

I do not wish to dogmatize on the revolutionary times through which we are living. I only wish to exhort the students to get in touch with those who really know the situation to determine when the moment is, what his responsibility is, and what the necessary reply is. Personally, I feel that we are fast approaching zero hour for the Colombian Revolution. But this only the proper authorities, the workers and farmers, can say. If the students "rise to the popular class," without any sense of paternalism, with more of a spirit of learning than of teaching, they will be able to judge objectively the historic moment.

It would, however, be fruitless and unfortunate if the Colombian students, who have been the spark of the Revolution, remain on the sidelines for any reason, whether for lack of information, egoism, irresponsibility, or fear. We hope that the students reply to their country's call in this crucial moment of its history, and that to do this they dispose themselves to hear and follow this call with unqualified generosity.

14. Building Up the Internal Organization

The agitational phase of the revolutionary process which the United Front has quickly brought about is nearly at an end. The organization, although widespread throughout the country, is still rudimentary. The work of extending the organization must be complemented by efforts to build it up from within. Provisional commands of the United Front have been created practically all over the country. These commands have taken three different forms. The first is the homogeneous command of the organized groups that participate, formally or informally, in the United Front (the M.O.E.C., the Communist Party, the Popular Nationalist Vanguard, the M.R.L., the Anapo, the Christian Democratic Party, and so forth). The second is the mixed command composed of elements from the previously mentioned groups and elements of the non-aligned. The third is the homogeneous command composed of the non-aligned in other groups.

Of these three types the most common is the second. The least organized is the command of the non-aligned. The United Front has established as a primary step the organization of the non-aligned. This designation seems too negative, since the "non-aligned" in the composed commands want very much to align themselves with the United Front and the Colombian Revolution. Many of them, in the grass roots, say that they belong to the United Front, but this is ambiguous since the United Front is also composed of other groups which they had no desire to join up to now, nor can they be obliged to join.

Some feel that it is necessary to form a new party of the non-aligned in order to become a part of the United Front. However, the non-aligned have no common philosophy; they are united by the platform, by the person of Camilo Torres, by the tactic of active abstention, and by the steadfast decision to seize power for the popular class. These elements would be basic to the constitution, not of a party, but of a movement which would permit the harmonious assimilation of the non-aligned so that they may thus participate in the United Front. From this follows the necessity of forming commands of non-aligned and of strengthening the group of non-aligned in the mixed commands. The final decision on the form of organization of the non-aligned, they themselves must furnish before the United Front convention.

In any case, the present need is to strengthen the existing commands. Those not formed in the grass roots (of simple farmers and workers) have been called provisional commands. Their main task is to organize the grass-root commands and have them name the definitive neighborhood, district, factory, municipal, and department commands. In addition to the special assignments that the provisional commands must handle according to the needs of each area, there are general assignments which must be carried out throughout the country, such as that previously mentioned of organizing grass-root commands, and the no less important task of stimulating and supporting the associated bodies (of workers, farmers, and students) in all their replevinary activities, trying to orient them towards the definitive struggle for the take-over of power for the popular class.

All the commands must devote themselves to the formation of leaders through special courses, command meetings, and dissemination of the platform. At this point we must sacrifice quantity for quality. To accomplish the assignments one good street, district, or factory command is preferable to several bad commands. The popular visage of the Colombian Revolution will not arise simply from the mass demonstrations. Each Colombian revolutionary should find a group of friends, neighbors, or co-workers with whom he could form a command group with the previously mentioned objectives. There is no need to await orders from above. In this way the United Front will acquire its own life, independent of the attitudes which the provisional leaders assume. The attitudes of these leaders should conform to the wish of the masses. Towards the end of this year or the beginning of next, true representatives of the people, at a large popular convention, will elect the national command of the United Front to determine the tactics for the elections and for the take-over of power.

XXII.

CALL TO THE COLOMBIAN PEOPLE

For many years the poor of our country have awaited the battle cry to throw themselves into the final struggle against the oligarchy.

At those moments when the desperation of the people was extreme, the ruling class always found a way to fool the people, to distract them, pacifying them with new formulas which always had the same end: the suffering of the people and the well-being of the privileged caste. When the people sought a leader and found one in Jorge Eliécer Gaitán, the oligarchy murdered him. When the people sought peace, the oligarchy sowed violence in the country. When the people could no longer tolerate this violence and organized guerrillas to take power, the oligarchy staged a military operation so that the misled guerrillas would become involved. When the people called for democracy, they were again fooled by a plebiscite and a National Front which imposed the dictatorship of the oligarchy.

Now the people will no longer believe. The people do not believe in the elections. The people know that the legal means have been exhausted and that no means remain but to arm. The people are desperate and resolved to risk their lives so that the next generation of Colombians will not be enslaved. So that the sons of those who are willing to give their lives may have an education, a roof over their heads, clothing, food, and above all *dignity*. So that future Colombians will have a country of their own, free of North American jurisdiction.

Any sincere revolutionary must realize that armed struggle is the only means that remains. However, the people are waiting for the leaders to give, by their example and their presence, the battle cry.

I wish to tell the Colombian people that the moment has come. That I have not betrayed you. That I have gone from city to town campaigning for the unity and organization of the popular class for the take-over of power. That I have asked that we all devote ourselves to these objectives, even at the risk of death.

Now everything is ready. The oligarchy wants to stage another farce of an election: with candidates whom they renounced and now accept, with bipartisan committees, with a renovation movement based on ideas and personalities who are not only old but who have betrayed the people. What more are we waiting for, Colombians?

I have joined the armed struggle. I plan to continue the struggle from the Colombian mountains with a weapon in my hand until power has been won for the people. I have joined the Army of National Liberation because in it I found the same ideals as those of the United Front. Because I found the desire for and realization of a unity within the grass roots, without regard to party or religious differences, without any spirit of antagonism among the various revolutionary elements, without bossism. Because I found that it seeks to liberate the people from the exploitation of the oligarchy and of imperialism. That it will not lay down its arms while the power is not wholly in the hands of the people. That in its objectives it accepts the platform of the United Front.

All patriotic Colombians ought to place themselves on a war footing. Little by little experienced guerrillas will appear all over the country. Meanwhile, we must be alert. We must gather arms and ammunition, seek guerrilla training, confer with one another, gather clothing, drugs, and provisions, and prepare ourselves for a prolonged struggle.

Let us make small strikes against the enemy wherever victory seems assured. Let us test all those who call themselves revolutionaries and weed out the traitors. Let us not hesitate to act, but let us not be impatient. In a prolonged war everyone will have

202

to take part in the action at some point. The important thing is that at that precise point everyone will be equipped and ready. There is no need for everyone to do everything; we must divide the work. The militants of the United Front must be the vanguard of initiative and action. Let us have patience in the confidence and expectation of final victory.

The people's struggle must be a national struggle. We have already begun, for the march is long.

Colombians: we must not hesitate to respond to the call of the people and of the Revolution.

Militants of the United Front: let us make our assignments realities:

For the unity of the popular class, unto death!

For the organization of the popular class, unto death!

For the seizure of power for the popular class, unto death!

Unto death because we have decided to continue to the end. Unto victory because a people that is devoted unto death always obtains its victory.

Unto final victory with the assignments of the Army of National Liberation:

Not one step in retreat!

Liberation or death!

SOURCES

I. THE MODERN UNIVERSITY AND SOCIAL PROBLEMS: presented at the First Seminar of University Chaplains, held in Bogotá in September 1956.

II. THE STANDARD OF LIVING IN BOGOTA: appeared in *Asociación Venezolana de Sociología,* a publication of the Sixth Latin American Congress of Sociology, held in Caracas, April 7–14, 1961.

III. LAND EXPLOITATION AND LAND REFORM: published in *Jueves de El Espectador,* August 11, 1960.

IV. STRUCTURING AN AUTHENTIC LATIN AMERICAN SOCIOLOGY: presented at the First Latin American Conference on Schools and Departments of Sociology, held in Buenos Aires, September 24–29, 1961.

V. THE STRUCTURE AND ROLE OF THE UNIVERSITY

1. *The Chaplain and the Rector:* summary of a report in *La Nueva Prensa,* June 30, 1962, of the events with which Father Torres is concerned in the next two articles.

2. *The Crisis of the University:* article in *El Espectador,* June 24, 1962.

3. *A Priest in the University:* editorial in *El Catolicismo,* June 28, 1962.

VI. URBANIZATION AND URBAN REFORM: presented to the National Seminary of University Staff of Colombia in Medellín, December 1962.

VII. THE PROBLEMS OF RURAL SOCIETY: presented at the First National Congress of Sociology, held in Bogotá, March 8–10, 1963.

VIII. THE BIDIMENSIONAL MAN: presented on Radio Sutatenza in Bogotá, September 1963.

IX. HOW PRESSURE GROUPS INFLUENCE THE GOVERNMENT: presented at the University of the Andes Alumni Association meeting, held in Bogotá in 1964.

X. SCIENCE AND THE DIALOGUE: written in Bogotá, June 1964.

XI. TWO SUBCULTURES: lecture presented in Bogotá, June 5, 1964.

XII. THE CHRISTIAN APOSTOLATE AND ECONOMIC PROGRAMMING: presented at the Second International Congress of Pro Mundi Vita, in Louvain, Belgium, September 1964.

XIII. CRITICISM AND SELF-CRITICISM: published in *El Espectador,* December 1964.

XIV. LETTER TO BISHOP RUBEN ISAZA: reply written on April 19, 1965, to the Auxiliary Bishop of Bogotá.

XV. PLATFORM OF THE UNITED FRONT OF THE COLOMBIAN PEOPLE: published in *Frente Unido,* February 1965.

XVI. COMMUNISM IN THE CHURCH?: interview which appeared in *La Hora,* May 1965.

XVII. POSSIBILITIES FOR THE LEFT: interview published in *La Gaceta,* May 1965.

XVIII. EXPROPRIATING CHURCH PROPERTY: interview published in *La Republica,* June 21, 1965.

XIX. LAICIZATION: statement published in *El Tiempo,* June 25, 1965, explaining the reasons for his request for laicization, which was made in a letter to Luís Cardinal Concha the day before.

XX. CROSSROADS OF THE CHURCH IN LATIN AMERICA: the conclusion of this undated document would seem to indicate that it was written around the time of the author's laicization, although it deals with a previous modification of his thoughts on charity which he sent to Coadjutor Bishop Isaza in April 1965.

XXI. THE UNITED FRONT: editorials published in *Frente Unido*.

    1. Why I Am Not Going to the Elections: August 26, 1965.

    2. Message to the Christians: August 26, 1965.

    3. Message to the Communists: September 2, 1965.

    4. Assignments: September 2, 1965.

    5. Message to the Military: September 9, 1965.

    6. Message to the Non-Aligned: September 16, 1965.

    7. Message to the Trade Unions: September 23, 1965.

    8. Father Torres Speaks: Referring to a statement made by Luís Cardinal Concha, Father Torres expressed his confidence in the ability of the Colombian Church to dedicate itself to the service of the poor. In a statement to Cadena Radial Caracol and a report to *El Espectador,* Father Torres pointed out that the Vatican asked the Colombian hierarchy to speak with him before imposing any sanction on him. The Cardinal's declaration censured Camilo Torres, the publishing of his thesis on the Colombian socio-economic situation, and his invitation to form a United Front of the People. He also held that Father Torres could not return to the practice of his priesthood. This article, appearing on September 30, 1965, takes up this last point.

    9. Message to the Peasants: October 7, 1965.

    10. Organizing the Non-Aligned: October 7, 1965.

    11. Message to the Women: October 14, 1965.

    12. The Platform and the Revolution: October 14, 1965.

    13. Message to Students: October 21, 1965.

    14. Building Up the Internal Organization: October 21, 1965.

XXII. CALL TO THE COLOMBIAN PEOPLE: appeared in *Christianismo y Revolución,* Buenos Aires, September 21, 1966.